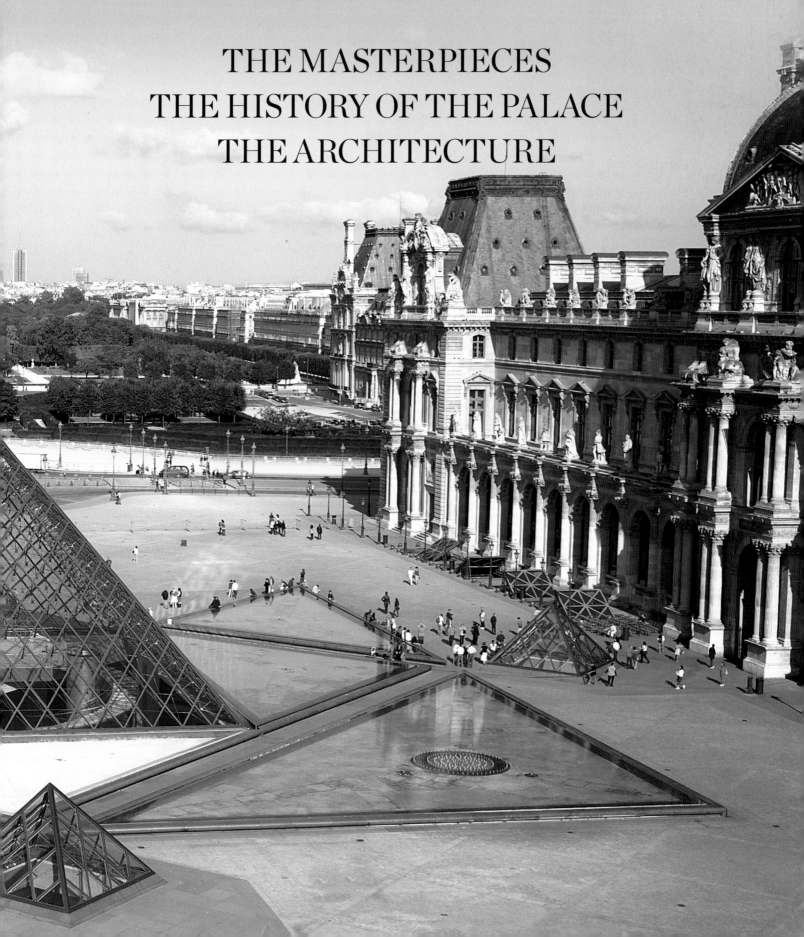

All the Louvre

THE MASTERPIECES
THE HISTORY OF THE PALACE
THE ARCHITECTURE

Contents

Preface

HENRI LOYRETTE
Chairman and Director of the Louvre Museum

What is the Louvre? An immense, unique museum whose collections range from 8 000 B.C. to 1848. These collections are constantly being improved and tell the story of humanity and its creativity. However, the Louvre is also an immense palace too, located at the heart of Paris and therefore at the heart of France, whose first stones were laid in 1190 during the reign of King Philippe Auguste to defend the capital. Since 1989 and the most recent archaeological excavations, visitors have been able to circulate freely in the moats of the medieval fortress, and walk along the bases of the old keep. When you visit the museum, you are also visiting the palace, for the two are inseparable. This visitor's guide combines three histories: the history of France, the history of architecture and the history of art, which the Louvre collections illustrate.

When you walk along the Grande Galerie, you can see masterpieces of Italian painting as well as cross a space, originally 460 metres long and designed to connect the Louvre to the Tuileries Palace, which no longer exists. As you travel around its 403 rooms, you can see the contributions of all the great men who made the Louvre, whose stories are told in this book. Take a walk outside, and realise that the Louvre is also a book on architecture, from the Middle Ages to the present day. The Louvre started as a home for kings and emperors, and was later converted into a museum. In the 18th century, the courts of the princes and sovereigns picked up the habit of exhibiting their collections, first to enlightened visitors, then to the general public. France was no exception: at the initiative of the Count d'Angiviller, part of the royal collections emigrated to the Louvre and the Grande Galerie during the reign of Louis XVI. It was not until 1793 that the Museum of Arts opened its doors and, little by little, the whole palace was dedicated to the arts. Coming from the Ancient East, Egypt, Greece and Rome, the antique collections sat alongside works from the Middle Ages, the Renaissance and modern times, using all techniques - paintings, sculptures and art objects. Thanks to the diversity and quality of these pieces, a real history of art can be seen in the rooms of the Louvre.

At the Louvre, nothing is set in stone, nothing is immobile: the museum is always expanding its collections, making room for contemporary art, and opening the big department of Islamic Arts... The story continues.

The great history of the
Louvre

Since it was founded at the end of the 12th century,
the Louvre has always been a place of expression for power.
More so than Blois, Fontainebleau, Versailles or the Élysée
Palace, it is the place where the history of France was
written, be it royal, revolutionary, imperial or republican.
At the palace, smaller and greater histories coexist without
really conflicting with each other: who has never dreamed of
hearing conspirers murmuring on the concealed staircases,
seeing poisoners from afar or meeting the kings' mistresses?
The Louvre is about the splendour of the grand balls as well
as the horror of the St. Bartholomew's Day massacre...

Timeline of the Palace

Philippe Auguste
(Reigned from 1180 to 1223)
1190: Philippe Auguste left
for the Crusades and ordered
the burghers of Paris to build
a wall around Paris.

Charles V
(Reigned from 1364 to 1380)
Transformation of the Louvre
by Raymond du Temple for Charles V.
Construction and decoration of the
"grande vis" ("great staircase").

François I
(Reigned from 1515 to 1547)
1528: destruction of the Grosse
Tour on the orders of François I.
1546: start of work on the new
Renaissance main building by Pierre
Lescot for François I, West Wing.

Henri II
(Reigned from 1547 to 1559)
1550: Jean Goujon sculpted the
caryatids of the great hall.
1554: Jean Goujon sculpted the
reliefs in the attic of the West Wing.

Charles IX
(Reigned from 1560 to 1574)
1560-1565: construction and
decoration of the South Wing.
1564: start of the construction of
the Tuileries Castle for Catherine
de Medici.
1566: first stone of the Petite
Galerie and a gallery connecting it
to the Tuileries, laid by Charles IX.

Henri IV
(Reigned from 1589 to 1610)
1595: start of the construction of
the Grande Galerie.

Louis XIII
(Reigned from 1610 to 1643)
1639: start of decoration of the
Clock Pavilion by Lemercier.

Louis XIV
(Reigned from 1643 to 1715)
1660: plan by Le Vau for the Louvre.
1661-1663: construction of the
South Wing (Galerie d'Apollon)
1662-1664: decoration of the
Galerie d'Apollon directed by Le Brun.
1665: Bernin's trip to Paris.
He lays the first stone of his east
façade for the Louvre.
1667: start of work on the Colonnade.
1668: expansion of the South Wing.
1672: pediment added to the
Colonnade. The Académie Française
moves into the Louvre.
1674: Louis XIV leaves the Louvre
permanently.

Louis XV
(Reigned from 1715 to 1774)
1756: clearing of the Colonnade.
1774-1789: Count d'Angiviller's
Museum project.

Convention (1792-1795)
1793: opening of the
Museum in the Grande Galerie
of the Louvre.

Directorate (1795-1799)
1798-1799: work on the
apartments of Anne of Austria
for the Antiquities Museum.

Consulate (1800-1804)
1800: opening of the
Antiquities Museum in the
apartments of Anne of Austria.
1803: Napoleon Museum.

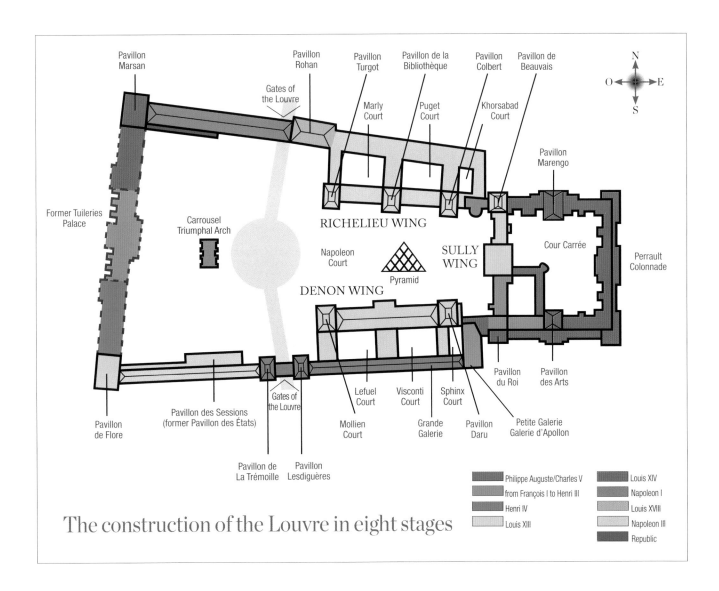

The construction of the Louvre in eight stages

Legend:
- Philippe Auguste/Charles V
- from François I to Henri III
- Henri IV
- Louis XIII
- Louis XIV
- Napoleon I
- Louis XVIII
- Napoleon III
- Republic

Map labels:
Pavillon Marsan, Pavillon Rohan, Pavillon Turgot, Pavillon de la Bibliothèque, Pavillon Colbert, Pavillon de Beauvais, Gates of the Louvre, Marly Court, Puget Court, Khorsabad Court, Pavillon Marengo, Former Tuileries Palace, Carrousel Triumphal Arch, RICHELIEU WING, Napoleon Court, Pyramid, SULLY WING, Cour Carrée, Perrault Colonnade, DENON WING, Pavillon du Roi, Pavillon des Arts, Lefuel Court, Visconti Court, Sphinx Court, Pavillon de Flore, Pavillon des Sessions (former Pavillon des États), Gates of the Louvre, Mollien Court, Grande Galerie, Pavillon Daru, Petite Galerie Galerie d'Apollon, Pavillon de La Trémoille, Pavillon Lesdiguères

N O E S

Napoleon I
(Reigned from 1804 to 1814)

1806: Carrousel Triumphal Arch. The Institute and artists are expelled from the Louvre.

1807: decoration of the attics of the Cour Carrée.

1808-1810: decoration of the Colonnade façade by Lemot and Cartellier.

1811-1814: decoration of the stairs on either side of the Colonnade.

Louis XVIII
(Reigned from 1814 to 1824)

1819-1824: painting of the ceilings (Salle Duchâtel, Rotonde de Mars).

1821: arrival of the Venus de Milo.

Charles X (1824-1830)

1827: opening of the Charles X Museum, first floor of the Cour Carrée.

Louis-Philippe
(Reigned from 1830 to 1848)

1831-1833: completion of the decoration of the future Campana Gallery.

1847: arrival of the first Assyrian antiquities.

Second Republic
(1848-1852)

1848: decision to complete the Louvre.

1851: inauguration of the Cour Carrée, the Salle des Sept Cheminées and the Galerie d'Apollon, restored by Duban.

1852: Start of work on the Napoleon Court by Visconti.

Napoleon III
(Emperor from 1852 to 1870)

1857: inauguration of the buildings in the Napoleon Court.

1861: demolition of the Pavillon de Flore.

1863: Napoleon III Museum. Presentation of the Campana collection at the Louvre. The Victory of Samothrace enters the Louvre.

Third Republic (1870-1940)

1871: Commune of Paris. Fire at the Tuileries. The Ministry of Finances moves into the Richelieu Wing.

1875-1878: reconstruction of the Flore and Marsan Pavilions.

1882: demolition of the Tuileries.

1905: inauguration of the Museum of Decorative Arts.

1926-1938: Director Henri Verne establishes a reorganisation plan for the museum.

Fifth Republic (since 1958)

1964: moats dug in front of the Colonnade.

1981: decision to make the "Grand Louvre".

1989: inauguration of the 1st phase of work and the Pyramid. The Ministry of Finances leaves for Bercy.

2000: inauguration of the African, Asian, Australasian and American art rooms at the Sessions Pavilion.

2012: inauguration of the new areas of the Department of Islamic Arts.

This chronology is taken from that published by Geneviève Bresc-Bautier in "The Louvre, Tale of a Palace", coéd. Musée du Louvre Éditions / Somogy, 2008.

The history of the Louvre Palace in 16 episodes

1190 A protective and defensive castle

In summer 1190, Philippe Auguste prepared to go to the Crusades after having put an end to the claims of Henry Plantagenet, Duke of Normandy and King of England. Before leaving his homeland, the King ordered the Parisians to protect their city; a wall was therefore built on both banks of the Seine and protected the city from any possible Anglo-Norman attacks. Construction began immediately and ended circa 1205.

As well as this development work, the sovereign had a fortress built to the West of Paris, to strengthen the city's defences: the Louvre was born. The first castle was a purely defensive building that had no real main building. It was the headquarters of a garrison and an arsenal. Placed outside of the walls, the castle was surrounded by spaces which were not heavily built up. As the decades passed, a suburb emerged along the future Rue Saint-Honoré, which would develop during the second half of the 13th century. A populated, rapidly developing neighbourhood was therefore placed under the Louvre's protection.

1356 The Louvre at the heart of the city ▲

The early 14th century was a difficult period for the kingdom of France, marked by the end of the Capetian dynasty and the Valois' accession to the throne. This was contested by England, which demanded the crown for its own king, Edward III: in 1337, the Hundred Years' War began. Paris, which was the biggest city in Europe at the time with 200 000 inhabitants, developed considerably but found itself powerless against the English threat. The construction of a new wall began under the leadership of Étienne Marcel in 1356. It enclosed the Louvre within the city, so it lost its advanced defensive function.

The reign of Charles V was a turning point in the long conflict between France and England, as the King managed to re-conquer most of the territory France had lost. The last decades of the 14th century saw Paris emerge as an economic and artistic superpower and unrivalled cultural centre. The transformed Louvre was at the heart of the city and the kingdom.

The Limbourg brothers
The Very Rich Hours of the Duke of Berry
The month of October with a depiction of the Louvre castle [detail]
Circa 1440-1450, painting on vellum, 29 x 21 cm.
Condé Musem, Chantilly,

1527 The King of France moves into the Louvre ▸

The late 15th and early 16th centuries were marked by the Wars of Italy. While Marignan secured victory for François I in 1515, Pavie's defeat in 1525 spelled the end of France's ambitions. In 1527, after spending a year in captivity in Madrid, the sovereign decided to move to Paris, abandoning the Loire Valley and the castles built at the start of his reign. The Louvre was the only building in his capital that offered a suitable home. As an art-lover and patron, the King amassed riches and artworks in Fontainebleau, Saint-Germain-en-Laye and Madrid Castle, in what would become the Bois de Boulogne forest. At the end of his life,

François I decided to rebuilt the Louvre in its entirety in order to signal his attachment to the capital. His death a year later meant he could not admire the new building, of which only the ground floor had been built. Designed by Pierre Lescot and decorated by Jean Goujon, the monument that would later be completed would be a model for the following generations.

Titian
François I, King of France
16th century, oil on canvas, 109 x 89 cm.
Louvre Museum, Paris.

1572 Catherine, mother of three kings, reigns at the Louvre ▾

Henri II did not start work on the Louvre again until 1549 and confirmed the appointment of Pierre Lescot to the position of project manager. Lescot finished the building in 1555 before embarking on even more ambitious new constructions. The King died accidentally during a tournament in 1559 and from then on, his widow, Catherine de

Medici, became the leading figure in the royal family until her death in 1589.
The era was marked by the accession to the throne of her three sons, François II, Charles IX and Henri III, who all died leaving no direct heir. She played a leading role in starting the Wars of Religion, which culminated on 24 August 1572 with the St. Bartholomew's Day

massacres, which reached as far as the heart of the Louvre, in the royal apartments. In Paris, the Queen Mother began the construction of the Tuileries Palace and its vast garden in 1564. The construction work was soon abandoned and would only be completed by Louis XIV, a century later.

French School
Ball held on the 24th of September 1581 at the court of Henri III in the Louvre, on the occasion of the wedding of the Duke of Joyeuse and Marguerite of Lorraine
Circa 1581-1582, oil on copper, 41 x 65 cm.
Louvre Museum, Paris.

The newlyweds dance in the centre while Catherine de Medici points at them, sitting on the left between Henri III, under the royal dais, and Queen Louise of Lorraine.

1595 The Grand Louvre of Henri IV

The assassination of Henri III in 1589 spelled the end of the Valois and the arrival in power of Henri of Navarre, the first sovereign of the Bourbon family. After the Wars of Religion ended, Henri IV was able to enter Paris in 1594, a few weeks after his coronation in Chartres. In his capital, the King embarked on some major town planning projects: construction of the Pont-Neuf, Place des Vosges and Place Dauphine. He also set up an ambitious project to expand the Louvre and finish the Tuileries. He had the Louvre Palace connected to the Tuileries Castle by the Grande Galerie. His death in 1610 prevented him from completing this work. The young Louis XIII was too young to reign, so his mother, Marie de Medici, acted as regent. Conflicts soon erupted between mother and son, culminating in the assassination at the Louvre of Concino Concini, the Queen Mother's favourite, in 1617, by order of the young king. Having seized power, Louis XIII began a policy to consolidate the royal power, which he sought to concretise by beginning a new phase of expansion at the Louvre.

1670 The old Louvre expands to its final size ▾

During the first years of the reign of Louis XIV, the Fronde shook the capital and the royal family mainly stayed at Saint-Germain-en-Laye. The sovereign only began to take an interest in the Louvre again in 1655. The construction of the Galerie d'Apollon from 1661 onwards, to replace the Galerie du Roi built by Henri IV and destroyed in a fire, signalled the starting point of a vast project to finish the Cour Carrée. Le Vau was put in charge of this work. In 1660, the North and South Wings were finished. The work on the East Wing, entrusted to Bernin, was finally completed by Le Brun, Le Vau, D'Orbay and Claude Perrault from 1667 onwards. With the construction of a new façade in front of the South Wing, on the Seine side, the old Louvre expanded to its final size. At the same time, the ambitious project to clear the area around the palace and redevelop the neighbourhood could not be completed due to a lack of money. As he was unable to stay at the Louvre during the work, the King had the Tuileries completed between 1659 and 1665. When he moved permanently to Versailles, the work on the Louvre was abandoned.

Ciceri, based on a drawing by Hoffbauer
The Louvre Palace in 1663
19th century, engraving.
At the centre, we see the south façade of the Cour Carrée under construction with the façade by Le Vau; backing onto the Seine, the Petite Galerie (future Galerie d'Apollon); and along the Seine, the Grande Galerie. On the far right, we can see the Hôtel de Bourbon.

1754 Louis XV orders the completion of the Cour Carrée wings ▲

When his great-grandfather died in 1715, the young Louis XV returned to Paris and stayed at the Tuileries Palace until 1722, before returning to Versailles. Since it was abandoned by Louis XIV, the Louvre had remained unfinished, and the North and East Wings of the Cour Carrée as well as part of the South Wing remained uncovered; the old royal apartments were occupied by the various academic institutions, and the rest was converted into accommodation for civil servants and artists housed by the King. Urged to take action by the Parisians, who were scandalised by the state of the castle, in 1754 the sovereign ordered the wings surrounding the Cour Carrée to be completed: Jacques Gabriel and Jacques Germain Soufflot finished the top floor of the façades and added the roofs 70 years late... Alongside this work, the last houses that still occupied part of the centre of the court were demolished, as well as those located in front of the Perrault Colonnade: the Louvre finally formed a decisive bond with the surrounding neighbourhoods.

1774 Museum project by the Count d'Angiviller ▼

Having moved to Versailles, the King only rarely stayed at the Tuileries, and only the Queen sometimes spent the night there after attending nights at the opera. The redevelopment work consisted of installing part of the royal painting collections in the Grande Galerie at the heart of the palace, in order to make them accessible to members of the public who were interested. The Count d'Angiviller was in charge of supervising the project, which the painter Hubert Robert and the architect Jacques Germain Soufflot also worked on. Due to a lack of money, the affair dragged on and was not completed until the Revolution. Major projects to redevelop the neighbourhood between the Louvre and the Tuileries were planned, organised around the construction of a new opera house: due to a lack of time and money, none would become a reality. A few months before the fall of the monarchy, there were still plans for the construction of a Louis XVI square!

Jean Jacques Lagrenée the Younger, *Allegory on the Installation of the Museum in the Grande Galerie of the Louvre,* 1783, oil on canvas, 52 x 68 cm. Louvre Museum, Paris.
The Count d'Angiviller can be seen in portrait form.

Hubert Robert
Design for the Grande Galerie in the Louvre in 1796

1796, oil on canvas, 112 x 143 cm.
Louvre Museum, Paris.

1793

A revolution, a museum at the heart of the palace ▶

The revolutionary events did not cause any notable destruction of the Louvre and Tuileries buildings. Brought to Paris in October 1789, the royal family returned to the Tuileries Palace and settled there. They remained there until August 1792, when the Parisian attack forced the King to take refuge with the Assembly: the monarchy was then abolished. With its occupants removed, the palace became the headquarters of various institutions: the Assembly moved there in May 1793.

Several committees were based in the rest of the building: the Committee of Public Safety is the most famous, occupying a large portion of the Queen's old apartments, near to the committees of decrees, agriculture, the navy... Art also settled at the heart of the monument. Hubert Robert and Jacques Louis David presided over the installation of the Museum of Arts, which opened on 10 August 1793 in the temporarily renovated Grande Galerie. Once it had entered the palace, the museum would never leave.

Louis Charles Auguste Couder
Napoleon I visiting the Stairs of the Louvre under the Guidance of the Architects Percier and Fontaine

1833, oil on canvas, 177 x 135 cm.
Louvre Museum, Paris.

The Emperor is escorted by Count Daru and Vivant Denon.

1801

Napoleon Museum ◀

The First Consul Bonaparte already resided at the Tuileries Palace; he officially moved in there as Emperor in 1802. His main intervention affected the palace's immediate surroundings, since he began the construction of Rue de Rivoli, between Place de la Concorde and Places des Pyramides, in 1801. At the same time, the demolition work to clear the area around the

Tuileries spelled the end for the neighbourhood that separated the Emperor's official residence from the Louvre Palace. From 1806, the Carrousel Triumphal Arch, built by Charles Percier and Pierre François Fontaine, enclosed the new court of honour in the imperial complex.
Napoleon extensively developed the spaces reserved for the collections of the museum that bore his name, creating new galleries for the antiquities. The project to complete the indoor spaces in the Colonnade Wing was only partially achieved. In the Cour Carrée, he completed the developments that had been continued under Louis XV, and standardised the upper parts of the wings surrounding the space.

1826 Creation of the Charles X Museum ▸

When he returned to Paris in 1814, Louis XVIII moved into the Tuileries, to live in areas abandoned by the Emperor's entourage. The transformations that the King had ordered were restricted to modifications within the apartments: new furniture was put in place, and symbols that were too closely associated with the memory of the empire were removed and replaced by fleurs de lys...

On an architectural level, Louis XVIII carried on with the wing that Napoleon had started along the future Rue de Rivoli; the completion of the Pavillon Rohan temporarily marked the end of the major work on the Louvre in the first half of the 19th century. In the Rohan Wing, the King also had the last decorative elements added to the Cour Carrée, bringing an end to the work started nearly three centuries earlier! King Charles X, who was crowned ten years later, oversaw the completion of several indoor spaces in the Cour Carrée area. He created the rooms that bear his name and were designed to house the Egyptian collections, of which Champollion was the first curator.

Joseph Auguste
The Jewel Room and Enfilade of Charles X Rooms
Circa 1835, oil on canvas, 100 x 81 cm.
Louvre Museum, Paris

Victor Joseph Chavet, *The Louvre of Napoleon III*
1857, oil on canvas, 212 x 222 cm, Louvre Museum, Paris.

1857 A monumental court joins the Louvre to the Tuileries ◂

As Emperor in 1852, Napoleon III decided almost immediately to finalise the redevelopment of the Louvre and Tuileries Palaces. The architects Visconti and then Lefuel were entrusted with the construction of the new buildings, while the prefect Haussmann was in charge of the definitive demolition of the neighbourhood that still separated the two buildings. The first stone was laid in 1853. In 1857, the new Louvre was finished and the Richelieu and Denon Wings stood on either side of the new monumental court which lay at the centre of the group.

In the following years, extensive redevelopment work was carried out to completely renovate certain parts of the old palace. The Grande Galerie was partly demolished then rebuilt; the transformation of the Tuileries Palace was begun but never finished. When the Franco-Prussian War broke out in 1870, the Louvre-Tuileries complex was at its largest in terms of surface area.

1883 The destruction of the Tuileries opens up a unique perspective ▸

On 4 September 1870, the Republic was proclaimed; Napoleon III, prisoner of the Prussians, left for exile in England. In Paris, under siege and bombed by enemy forces, people protected the works at the museum as best they could, and a number of pieces of furniture and decorative works adorning the rooms in the Tuileries Palace were stored away.

A few months later, the Commune began: the Parisians in revolt defended the city. Fighting was violent and resulted in immense destruction. On 23 May 1871, the Tuileries were set on fire. Their ruins would remind the Parisians of these dark days until the Chamber of Deputies voted to raze them to the ground in 1879. The demolition of the ruins started in 1883, opening the Louvre's perspective towards the garden, as far as L'Étoile.

In the interim, starting in 1874, the damaged parts of the Louvre which were not destined for demolition were restored: the Flore and Marsan Pavilions were rebuilt, and now stand at the west end of the complex.

The burnt ruins of the Tuileries Palace
Photograph, 1871

1964 Malraux has a moat dug in front of the Perrault Colonnade ▾

Moat in front of the Louvre colonnade built by Claude Perrault

With the demolition of the Tuileries, the Louvre took the shape that we know today. No particular architectural transformation was made to the building, outside of the sometimes major work to extend the museum further within the monument. While the building itself was not really affected, its environment underwent more radical changes. The old court of honour of the Tuileries Palace became a garden, which prolonged the landscaped space into the heart of the Louvre.

The palace was spared during the two world wars, and lay dormant in the following decades. André Malraux, first Minister of Culture appointed by the General de Gaulle, revived it in 1964 when he had a moat dug in front of the Perrault Colonnade, which may have been planned as early as the 17th century but had never been completed. It emphasised the building's façade line and gave it a more monumental aspect, as well as forming a separation between the Louvre and the city centre.

1989 The Pyramid, symbol of the Grand Louvre ▶

Louvre Pyramid built by Ieoh Ming Pei

When he announced that the Ministry of Finances was moving, on 26 September 1981, François Mitterrand laid the first stone of a vast project that would completely remodel the old palace and the museum between its walls. The project of the President of the Republic aimed to allocate the entire Louvre to the museum, doubling the surface area for the permanent collections while creating vast spaces for the public.

A clearly visible entrance was needed at the centre of the complex, beneath the Napoleon Court: the architect Ieoh

Ming Pei designed the Pyramid that would soon become the very symbol of the palace. On 30 March 1989, the whole building opened to the public. The new spaces were developed alongside a vast restoration campaign, culminating in the renovation and

cleaning of all of the Louvre's façades. The opening of the Richelieu Wing in 1993 made it possible to cover the three inner courts (Marly, Puget and Khorsabad) of the old Ministry of Finances and brought the Grand Louvre project to completion.

2012 In the Visconti Court, the revolution of Islamic Arts ▼

In the years that followed the inauguration of the Richelieu Wing in 1993, new areas of the palace were redeveloped and opened to the public, around the old stables of Napoleon III, in the Lefuel and Visconti Courts. In 1997, the opening of new rooms for the departments of Near Eastern Antiquities and then for Egyptian Antiquities temporarily signalled the end of the

major works. Alongside these indoor works, the Carrousel and Tuileries Gardens were redeveloped and restored, creating a closer link between the Louvre and "its" garden.

In 2012, the last remaining free spaces of the palace were redeveloped: rooms were opened in the Visconti Court, dedicated to Islamic arts amongst other things. The veil placed by the

architects Rudy Ricciotti and Mario Bellini over the collection areas marked the end of eight centuries of constructions and transformations associated with the spaces of the palace, perhaps provisionally.

3D simulation (cross-section) of the Visconti Court, where the Islamic arts collection is displayed.

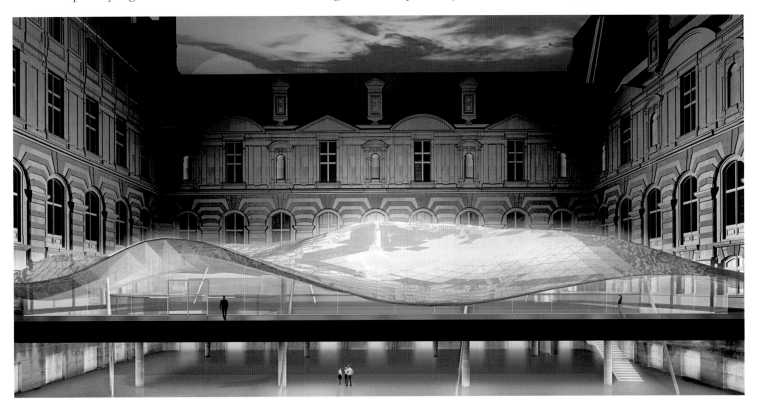

They built the Louvre

Jean-Pierre Dantan the Younger
Pierre Lescot
1833, marble, H. 92 cm. Versailles and Trianon Castle, Versailles.

1 Raymond du Temple
The great ancestor

Little is known about the man who was the main project manager for Charles V's Louvre. His name appeared for the first time in June 1359 in the registers of Notre-Dame in Paris, where he finished the chancel's enclosure. While the Louvre was his main work, he was also involved with the works on Hôtel Saint-Pol, another Parisian residence of Charles V, and the completion of Vincennes Castle, where he erected the Sainte-Chapelle. He died in the early years of the 15th century, in 1403 or 1404.

2 Pierre Lescot (1515-1578)
The favourite of François I and Henri II

He was the main architect of the Louvre during the Renaissance. François I commissioned him to make the wing that still bears his name, on 2 August 1546. Henri II confirmed him as project manager in 1549 to carry on with the work: he was the designer of the West and South Wings of the Cour Carrée and the Pavillon du Roi. The poet Ronsard, his friend, said that he excelled "in painting, drawing, mathematics and architecture". Lescot was the architect of the Innocents Fountain and Hôtel Carnavalet in Paris.

3 Jean Goujon
The best sculptor of his time

Little is known about the genius behind the decorations of the revived Louvre; his dates of birth and death are unknown. He became well-known from 1544 onwards for his work on decorating the jube at Saint-Germain-l'Auxerrois and was then entrusted with decorating the façades at the new Louvre. He then made the four caryatid figures of the great hall which occupies the ground floor of the new wing of the palace. He was the best sculptor of his time, and was also the author of the decorations at the Innocents Fountain built by Pierre Lescot.

Joseph Beaume
Jean Goujon
19th century, lithograph, 33.4 x 23.6 cm, Versailles and Trianon Castles, Versailles.

4 Philibert Delorme (circa 1510-1570)
Designer of the Tuileries

The architect and designer of part of the Tuileries Palace, he was the first to carry the title of Royal Architect. He came from a family of masons and was trained in Italy. He made his name by building Saint-Maur Castle at the edge of Paris. After he was spotted by the court, he built Anet Castle for Henri II, and the sovereign's funerary monument in Saint-Denis. Catherine de Medici entrusted him with the project to develop the Tuileries Palace, but it was too ambitious and was only partially completed.

Philibert Delorme
1545. National Museum of the Renaissance, Écouen.

5 **Jacques Lemercier** (1585-1654)
The Pavillon Sully

He was awarded the title of First Architect of the King in 1635. He built the Sully Pavilion and the Lemercier Wing for Louis XIII, and gave one of the sides of the Cour Carrée the dimensions that Louis XIV would keep for the other sides. He also made great religious buildings, including the Louvre Oratory, Sorbonne Chapel, Carmelite Church and Val-de-Grâce… For the Cardinal de Richelieu, Minister of Louis XIII, he built the Palais-Royal and Richelieu Castle, which has since been destroyed.

Philippe de Champaigne
Jacques Lemercier depicted in front of the Sorbonne Chapel
1644, oil on canvas, 97 x 75 cm. Versailles and Trianon Castles, Versailles.

6 **Charles Le Brun** (1619-1690)
The Galerie d'Apollon

The man who was made Director of the Royal Academy of Painting and Sculpture and the Gobelins factory in 1663, and First Painter of the King in 1664, was the most important artist during Louis XIV's reign. In fact, Le Brun spearheaded the King's cultural policy: he designed the decorations for the Galerie d'Apollon at the Louvre and worked on the project to develop the palace's new East Wing. After that, he was in charge of decoration at Versailles for thirty years, where he painted the vaults of the Mirror Gallery.

Nicolas de Largillière
Charles Le Brun, First Painter of the King
1683-1686, oil on canvas, 232 x 187 cm. Louvre Museum, Paris.

7 **Louis Le Vau** (1612-1670)
The south façade of the Cour Carrée

Le Vau must be considered as one of the originators of Classicism during the time of Louis XIV. Made First Architect of the King in 1654, he was the brilliant creator of Vaux-le-Vicomte for the Superintendent of Finances, Nicolas Fouquet. He then worked on completing the Cour Carrée at the Louvre and Tuileries Palace, and directed the works at Versailles until he died. His south façade of the Cour Carrée, facing the Seine, is a masterpiece of French Classicism with its rigour, simplicity and monumentality.

Anonymous
Louis Le Vau
1619-1684, oil on canvas, 152 x 126 cm. Versailles and Trianon Castles, Versailles.

8 **Claude Perrault** (1613-1688)
The east façade of the Louvre

The brother of the writer Charles Perrault, Claude was trained as a doctor and became a member of the Royal Academy of Sciences in 1666. He was mainly known as an architect, and member of the commission in charge of designing the new east façade of the Louvre after Bernin's project had been abandoned. He also designed the Paris Observatory and then worked on various constructions in Versailles. He died of an infection following the dissection of a camel at the Jardin des Plantes.

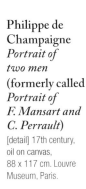

Philippe de Champaigne
Portrait of two men (**formerly called** *Portrait of F. Mansart and C. Perrault*)
[detail] 17th century, oil on canvas, 88 x 117 cm. Louvre Museum, Paris.

9 Charles Claude de Flahaut de La Billarderie, Comte d'Angiviller (1730-1810)

The promoter of the Antique style

A career soldier and friend of the young Louis XVI, the Count d'Angiviller was made Director General of the Buildings, Arts, Gardens and Factories of France in 1774. Passionate about town planning and architecture, he would promote the Antique style on the eve of the Revolution. Responsible for acquiring works for the Crown, he commissioned David to produce *The Oath of the Horatii*. D'Angiviller was also behind the project to install the royal collections in the Grande Galerie of the Louvre.
He died in exile in Altona (Hamburg).

Joseph Siffred Duplessis
Charles Claude de La Billarderie, Count d'Angiviller
18th century, oil on canvas,144 x 106 cm. Versailles and Trianon Castles, Versailles.

10 Hubert Robert (1733-1808)

The Museum's first curator

Trained in Paris and then Rome, where he stayed for eleven years, the painter Hubert Robert returned to France to occupy various positions that brought him close to the court. Accepted into the Royal Academy of Painting and Sculpture in 1766, he became the guardian of the King's paintings and was put in charge of the project to install the artworks in the Louvre's Grande Galerie. Incarcerated during the Terror and then freed, he returned to the Louvre, where he worked on developing the Central Museum. He was made curator of the museum in 1800.

Élisabeth Vigée-Le Brun
Hubert Robert
1788, oil on wood, 105 x 84 cm. Louvre Museum, Paris.

11 Jacques Louis David (1748-1825)

The creation of the Central Museum

Trained in the Vien's studio, David moved to the Louvre in 1782, living in an apartment that also acted as a studio. A member of the Royal Academy from 1783, he presented his *Oath of the Horatii* in the Louvre's Cour Carrée in 1785, a real manifesto for a new painting style, which would be bought by the King. Very attached to the revolutionary movement, David would vote for the death of Louis XVI before playing an important role in the creation of the Central Museum. He became Napoleon's favourite artist, and died in exile in Brussels.

Jacques Louis David
Portrait of the Artist
1794, oil on canvas, 81 x 64 cm. Louvre Museum, Paris.

12 Charles Percier (1764-1838) - Pierre François Fontaine (1762-1853)

The Empire style

The two architects met at Peyre's studio. From the Consulate onwards, they were inseparable and became the great representatives of the Empire style: they were responsible for the façades of the buildings on Rue de Rivoli, the completion of the Cour Carrée in the Louvre, the design of the Carrousel Arch and many developments in the palace. They created opera decorations and delivered models to the Sèvres factory.

Robert Lefèvre
Charles Percier
1807, oil on canvas, 86 x 54 cm. Versailles and Trianon Castles, Versailles.

Joseph Désiré Court
Pierre François Léonard Fontaine
19th century, oil on canvas, 130 x 97 cm. Versailles and Trianon Castles, Versailles.

13 **Dominique Vivant Denon** (1747-1825)
The man of collections

A diplomat and engraving artist, Denon was the leading figure in a crucial period, marked by the creation of the museum. A member of the expedition to Egypt and co-founder of the Egyptian Institute in Cairo in 1798, he worked on publishing the immense *Description of Egypt*. Close to Napoleon I, he was made Director of the Louvre Museum of Arts on 19 November 1802. He considerably expanded the collections with finds from all over Europe, but in 1815 he saw his work dispersed: he then handed in his resignation to the King.

Robert Lefèvre
Vivant Denon
1808, oil on canvas,
92 x 78 cm.
Versailles and Trianon
Castles, Versailles.

14 **Jean-François Champollion** (1790-1832)
Curator of Egyptian Antiquities

Born in Figeac, in Lot, Champollion passed much of his childhood in Grenoble before moving to Paris.
A student of Coptic and various ancient languages, from 1808 he took an interest in hieroglyphic writing, whose secret he deciphered fourteen years later, in 1822. A renowned scholar, in 1826 he was made head of the Egyptian collections at the Louvre, where he was the first curator. In 1828, he finally saw Egypt on a journey that lasted two years. He was made a professor at the College of France in 1831 and died a year later.

Léon Cogniet
Jean-François Champollion
1831, oil on canvas,
73.5 x 60 cm.
Louvre Museum,
Paris.

15 **Louis Tullius Joachim Visconti** (1791-1853) **- Hector Lefuel** (1810-1880)
The Napoleon Court

Just as Percier and Fontaine were inseparable from the Louvre of Napoleon I, Visconti and Lefuel were indissociable from the palace of Napoleon III. However, they took turns at the head of the immense construction project which began in 1852. Visconti designed the two wings on either side of the Napoleon Court, but premature death stopped him from carrying out his plans. Lefuel made them a reality, while considerably developing the decorative scheme for the building.

Théophile Vauchelet
Louis Visconti in front of the Louvre enlargement project
1854, oil on canvas. Carnavalet Museum, Paris.

Eugène Giraud
Caricature of Lefuel
1860, print. BnF, Paris.

16 **Ieoh Ming Pei** (born in 1917)
The Louvre Pyramid

An American of Chinese origin, Pei is the most striking figure in the modern Louvre. He was involved in making the new wing of the National Gallery in Washington, and was chosen in 1983 by François Mitterrand to design the new entrance to the Louvre and rework the palace's whole museum development. The opening of the Louvre Pyramid in 1989 established him as a celebrity. Well-loved by the museum world, he was also the author of the new building for the Museum of German History in Berlin and the Museum of Islamic Art in Doha (Qatar).

Ieoh Ming Pei
in front of the
Pyramid site in 1985

Five historical episodes in the life of the Louvre

"Kill them All!" cried the young King

The Protestant leaders, invited to Paris for the marriage of Henri of Navarre, fall into the trap set by the Queen.

Catherine de Medici was 53 years old. She had been looking after the affairs of the kingdom since the death of her husband, Henri II, in 1559. Her son, King Charles IX, was only 22. His health was fragile; he lived in a state of permanent anguish, suffering from devastating fits of hysterics and no longer able to bear anything, neither his mother, who suffocated him with her advice, her plots and her preference for his brother Henri nor this endless war between Catholics and Protestants in his kingdom. Although he was an extremely Catholic king, he was a passionate admirer of the Admiral of Coligny – to the extent that he called him "my father" –, who was none other than the leader of the Protestants. It must be said that the Admiral had everything the young king did not – authority, calmness under pressure and courage. After years of civil war and massacres, an attempt at a peace treaty had been signed in Saint-Germain in 1570. The Huguenots were allowed to enter Paris and it was decided that the King of Navarre, Henri,

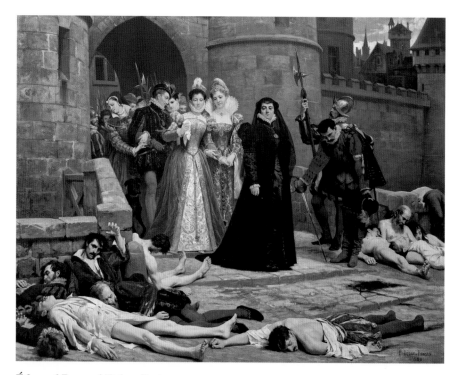

Édouard Bernard Debat-Ponsan
One Morning at the Door of the Louvre
1880, oil on canvas, 320 x 396 cm. Roger-Quillot Museum of Art, Clermont-Ferrand.

20

a Protestant, would marry the King's sister Margaret in Paris on 18 August. The confident Protestant leaders arrived from throughout France to witness this marriage. For Catherine, who hated and envied the virtuous Coligny, it was too good an opportunity to miss. Together with her second son Henri, her henchman and the future king Henri III, she decided to have the Admiral killed, without warning the young King Charles. Unfortunately, her roughneck soldier only managed to wound him. The Protestants, of whom there were a large number in the city, immediately demanded to know who was responsible. They soon found out, the King first, that the Queen Mother was involved. She panicked and gathered her supporters, her son Henri, the Duke of Guise and Birague, the new Garde des Sceaux together at the Louvre. There was only one solution, to massacre the Protestant leaders so they would no longer have to live under the threat of a new rebellion. The heat that day was stifling. The Queen feared her son's reaction to this assassination plan. Her advisor, the Italian Gondi, was responsible for explaining everything to the King. He rushed to him and told him that the Protestant leaders had decided to get rid of the Royal family and advised him to strike first. The King was shaken. His mother arrived next and drowned him under a stream of words,

The King summoned Henri of Navarre and commanded him to choose between Mass, death or the Bastille!

tears and threats. He could not take any more, no longer understood and did not want to hear any more. Suddenly he shouted "Kill them all, don't leave a single one alive to reproach me!" Kill them all! Words spoken in haste! The Protestants were well armed, so they needed men. They found them in the Paris militia, these bourgeois, these soldiers dreaming of doing battle with the Huguenot party. Their leader Claude Marcel was enthusiastic – blood would finally flow. During the afternoon, the houses of Protestants were marked with a cross. The men were told nothing and it was not until the following morning that they would find out the reason for their mobilisation. At the Louvre, no one slept that night. In the morning the Queen Mother could take no more, panicked and had someone tell Guise to abandon the operation. It was too late. The Admiral had already been killed by the

troops meant to be guarding him and his body had been thrown out of the window. His head was taken to the Louvre as a trophy and his corpse was dismembered by the mob. Catherine flew into a rage and launched the troops. At the Palace, Henri of Navarre was summoned by the very troubled King, who ordered him to choose between Mass, death or the Bastille! Henri wanted to survive. He chose Mass, i.e. conversion. There would always be time to recant once he was free. In the Louvre Palace, the Protestant gentlemen and their staff were brought into the courtyard before the King and Queen, who were standing on the balcony, and executed by the Swiss troops with clubs and weapons or mercilessly run through with halberds. The King himself, shot from a window and joined in the party. In the Louvre, people were running from window to window so as not to miss any of the slaughter. Thousands of men, women and children died and were thrown onto carts, to be tipped into the Seine. It was not long until people were killing for the sake of pillaging. The Queen Mother understood that it was time for the violence to stop. As for the Wars of Religion, they continued for a long time...

François Dubois
Saint Bartholomew's Day Massacre,
25 August 1572, oil on panel, 154 x 94 cm.
Art and History Museum, Lausanne.

25 JUNE 1610 Funeral wake for the body of Henri IV, attended by the young Louis XIII

Covered with a gold sheet, the King lay in the Salle des Cariatides

Henri IV, assassinated by Ravaillac, is presented at the Louvre.
A long procession of dignitaries pay him their last respects.

The horse-drawn carriage entered the Cour Carrée of the Louvre at high speed and stopped in front of the doors leading to the Grand Degré staircase. Mr de Montbazon and the Duke of Epernon, who had been at the Arsenal with Henri IV, climbed out quickly, holding the King's body at arm's length. "He is only injured", announced the Duke of Epernon to the frightened servants. The King was dead, assassinated by Ravaillac in the centre of Paris a few minutes earlier. It was 14 May 1610 and a child barely nine years of age had just lost his father and had to accede to the French throne.

The young Louis XIII did not take part in the funeral ceremonies which took place at the Louvre over the next month. However, there was a large crowd of people and the decor was sombre, expressing the sorrow and gravity of the situation. The King's body was placed in his room on the first floor of the palace and could not yet be viewed; however, in accordance with tradition, a wax effigy of the sovereign was placed in the large ground floor hall, the Salle des Cariatides and people gathered in front of this throughout the day. Constant prayer vigils were held, with the major Court dignitaries filing in and out of the hall with around a dozen gentlemen from their staff. Throughout the time the recumbent statue was on display, the supper table continued to be laid between two pillars, at the end of the Hall, without any changes to the usual protocol. The meal was served as if for the late King, although the dishes were not announced aloud so as not to disturb the celebration of the masses taking place at the same time. Almost one hundred times a day priests came to say prayers at one of the twelve altars created under the crosses in the Hall.

However, after a few weeks, the effigy was removed from the Salle des Cariatides. Heavy black drapes with thick velvet borders were hung there, and also on the Cour Carrée and the main façade of the palace. The King's body, in its coffin, was then placed in the centre of the room, supported by trestles, in the same place as his sculptured image had been. A large gold sheet embossed with a white silk cross covered the remains, and the crown was placed on the coffin, where the head was. A very solemn service was prepared.

On 25 June 1610, the young Louis XIII

François Quesnel, according to Isaac Briot
Portrait of the Highest, Most Mighty, Most Excellent Prince Henry the Great
17th century, intaglio, 33.3 x 24.2 cm
The body of Henri IV on display at the Louvre.

Charles Gustave
Housez
*Assassination
of Henri IV and
arrest of Ravaillac
on 14 May 1610*
1860, oil on canvas,
140 x 118 cm.
National Museum of the
Château of Pau.

There were constant prayer vigils, with each major court dignitary devoting two hours to them.

came to pay his last respects to his father the King. For the occasion, a long procession formed from the Longueville Mansion, where the young King still lived, to the Louvre Palace, which had been decorated for the occasion. The general Provost, wearing mourning dress, began the march accompanied by his archers, who were dressed in black under their armour. Then came around one hundred gentlemen, most of them soldiers and each carrying a ceremonial war hammer. Then came members of the aristocracy, members of parliament and officers, all wearing mourning dress, followed by Cardinal de Joyeuse and Cardinal de Sourdy who were escorting the child. The child was wearing violet mourning dress, with a long coat whose five tails were held behind him by five of the highest dignitaries of the Kingdom. The cortege left at midday and arrived at about 1 pm in front of the doors of the Louvre, where a huge crowd was waiting. Louis XIII entered the Salle des Cariatides, approached the coffin to sprinkle holy water and knelt down beside his late father. The ceremony lasted almost two hours, at the end of which the young King retired to his apartments. The body of the late king would not leave the Louvre until a few days later, but his son would not see it again. In accordance with tradition, a ruling King did not witness the burial of his predecessor. In the words of Malherbe, who summarised the events, "fate scoffs at kings in life and in death, so they remember that they are men".

10 AUGUST 1793 The Central Museum of the Arts is opened to the public

Masterpieces reserved solely for the artists?

After lengthy discussions, it was agreed that the general public could enter the museum on twelve days a month.

On the day of its opening, the Louvre was already celebrating an anniversary, that of the attack on the Tuileries Palace, one year earlier, which had led to the arrest of the royal family and hastened the fall of the monarchy. The birth of the museum had in fact occurred four years earlier, on 21 June 1789, when the States General had decided to create a museum to exhibit the masterpieces of the Crown's collections. Two years later, on 26 May 1791, the Constituent Assembly decided to install the Museum at the Louvre.

On this day, 10 August 1793, the place the public discovered was nothing like the current museum. Firstly, it only occupied a small part of it, as the only accessible areas were the Salon Carré and part of the Grande Galerie. Secondly, its collections were still embryonic, as the exhibits were mainly paintings together with a few sculptures placed there for mainly decorative purposes. Finally, the people who visited the museum had nothing in common with today's public, as they were mainly artists and a few art-lovers. It would be another two centuries before foreign tourists started to flock there.

The Grande Galerie was still undergoing major work. The death of Henri IV, in 1610, had left it unfinished and no work had been carried out to complete it. The ambitious decor of the vault, entrusted to Poussin, never progressed beyond the preparatory drawings.

The painter Hubert Robert then attempted to clean, reinforce and

Hubert Robert
The Grande Galerie at the Louvre
Between 1794 and 1796,
oil on canvas, 37 x 41 cm.
Louvre Museum, Paris

It was not until David arrived that a little order was installed in the collections. The museum became an instant success.

complete the huge nave, then 460 metres long. His attempts to create lighting from above would not be achieved until later by the architects of Napoleon I. In the meantime, paintings were placed side-by-side in the long gallery, originally in no particular order, in accordance with the tradition of 18th century princely galleries: the Italian works next to the Flemish, the 15th century side-by-side with the 17th. It was not until several months later that the painter David intervened and imposed a bit of order by classifying works according to their school.

The museum was less accessible than it is today and a difficult decision had to be made between those who wanted to open it to all members of the public, as the archaeologist Quatremère de Quincy suggested it and those who preferred enjoyment of the collections to be reserved solely for artists, which is what Jacques Louis David wanted. The museum chose a clever compromise, with opening times divided into ten-day periods, during which six days were strictly reserved for artists and foreign visitors, three were reserved for Parisians and the tenth and last day was devoted to cleaning. Large numbers of people visited and the museum was an instant success: the most beautiful paintings from the Royal collections were there, including works by Corrège, Titian, Rubens, Poussin and Leonardo da Vinci. The *Monna Lisa* was not there, as until 1797 it was at the Superintendency of the King's buildings and was unknown to art lovers. As well as the King's paintings, there were works seized from emigrant families and works belonging to the Church, as well as paintings belonging to the former Royal Academy. The collection as a whole offered an important glimpse into Western pictorial creation from the end of the Middle Ages to the 18th century.

The collections were extended over the following years and the public constantly discovered new arrivals, which would be exhibited in recently opened areas. For example, the drawings by the King's former staff were exhibited in the Galerie d'Apollon from 1797, soon joined by the sculptured stone and bronzes of the Crown transferred there from the furniture depository on Place de la Concorde. Antiques, of which there were few initially, increased in number from 1797 and new rooms were opened up for them on the ground floor of the palace. Barely five years after it opened, the current museum had begun to take shape under the original institution.

Hubert Robert
The Hall of the Seasons at the Louvre
Circa 1802-1803, oil on canvas, 37 x 46 cm.
Louvre Museum, Paris.

23 MAY 1871 The Tuileries on fire!

The Palace of the Kings, a casualty of the civil war

The Communards decide to set fire to the symbols of a despised power.
For the Louvre, a huge perspective opens up towards the West.

The Tuileries Palace, born from the desire of Queen Catherine de Medici, was the work of three successive architects, Philibert Delorme, Jean Bullant and Androuet du Cerceau. Her son-in-law Henri IV decided to connect it to the Louvre, joining it via the Grande Galerie.

When, under Napoleon, it once again became the sovereign's residence, following an interlude at Versailles, the palace underwent permanent internal transformations.

In January 1871, after the Germans had destroyed the troops of its last occupant, Napoleon III, and taken him

Inside view of the Hall of Marshals at the Tuileries Palace, circa 1873
Château of Versailles and Château of Trianon, Versailles.

prisoner, Paris was surrounded and bombarded but refused to surrender. Bismarck then decided to starve it and as a result 25,000 cats were eaten! On 28 January, a 21-day armistice was signed with the Prussians. Those who wanted order, i.e. surrender, were agitating in the city against the revolutionaries who wanted to resist at all costs. General elections were held in France on 8 February, giving victory to peace. There would therefore be negotiations with the Prussians. Rather Bismarck (the German Chancellor) than Blanqui (the revolutionary leader) was the credo of the Paris bourgeois. Thiers, the head of government, negotiated an agreement which authorised the Germans to occupy part of the city for a few months and required the Paris national guard, which had set itself up as a "Commune", to surrender the 200 cannons it possessed. Categorical refusal. On 18 March, Thiers decided to resort to force. He sent General Lecomte to collect the cannons, but his troops fraternised with the rioters and he himself was shot.

Thiers was frightened by the behaviour of his Paris troops, evacuated the city and took refuge in Versailles. Versailles, the symbol of the hated monarchy! On 26 March, the Paris Council elections were won by revolutionaries... Not suspecting anything, the Communards attempted a sortie towards Mount Valerian, which was held by the Versaillais (government troops). It was a complete failure and their leaders were

"General" Jules Bergeret set up a device consisting of gunpowder, liquid tar, turpentine and petroleum.

taken prisoner and shot. Thiers then launched the regular army against these Communards whom he detested; he was responsible for a massacre out of all proportion with the violence committed by his adversaries. On 21 May, bloody week began under the alarmed yet delighted eyes of the Prussians. Barricades were erected. On 22 May, the Versaillais occupied a line which went from Ternes to Montparnasse station. Fire was soon being used: "Rather Moscow than Sedan" was the saying among the Communards, referring to the city of Moscow set alight by the Russians when Napoleon arrived. Calmly and coldly, they attacked the symbols of a despised regime and the buildings which had made the city famous.

"General" Jules Bergeret (he was actually a proofreader), who had just left the Bourbon Palace, withdrew to the Tuileries, but had to abandon the castle due to the advance of the Versaillais. Together with a policeman, Étienne Boudin, and a butcher's boy, Bénot, he set up a device consisting of gunpowder, liquid tar, turpentine and petroleum, and placed the whole thing under the peristyle of the central pavilion. The building burned for three days and three nights, from 23 to 26 May, the bronzes melted and the marble was reduced to dust. The author Emile Zola witnessed the fire, "The roofs, yawning as does the earth in regions where volcanic agencies prevail, were seamed with great cracks through which the raging sea of fire beneath was visible [...] the petroleum with which the floors and hangings had been soaked gave the flames an intensity such that the ironwork of the balconies was seen to twist and writhe in the convolutions of a serpent, and the tall monumental chimneys, with their elaborate carvings, glowed with the fervour of live coals [...]." Paris was ablaze, but Thiers' victory was complete. The wounded, women and children were shot, a total of 20,000 people. The Commune had "only" massacred 500 prisoners. During the following years, people came to admire the sight of these ruins, as the use of petroleum had turned them strange colours, greys, rich bronzes, giving a surprising impression of age. Théophile Gautier thought that they resembled ancient ruins. Should the Tuileries be rebuilt? The matter ended with committees. After a number of projects, in 1882 the decision was made to destroy the ruins. An entrepreneur, Aristide Picard, was appointed to sell some of the ruins. The Louvre received some remains, including an arch which is currently located in the Marly Court. Around one hundred items are spread around the world, pieces of architecture which evoke the splendour of this château.

Anonymous
Fire at the Tuileries, 24 May 1871
Carnavalet Museum, Paris.

30 MARCH 1989 Inauguration of the Napoleon Hall and the Pyramid

The symbol of a new era

François Mitterrand wanted the Pyramid, ignoring all opposition. The future would prove him right. The entrance it marks has been crossed by millions of visitors, making the Louvre the most popular museum in the world.

The official inauguration of the Louvre Pyramid by François Mitterrand, President of the Republic, and Jack Lang, Minister for Culture, almost marked the end of a controversy which had lasted several years. When, in 1981, the newly elected François Mitterrand announced his desire for an authoritative extension to the Louvre Museum within the area then occupied by the Finance Ministry, the reaction was almost unanimously positive. The choice of Ieoh Ming Pei, known for the creation of the remarkable new wing of the National Gallery in Washington, was also hailed by the press and cultural circles. The idea of constructing a new buil-ding to house the new museum entrance, on the other hand, caused controversy. How could they think of placing modern architecture in the heart of the place which, more than any other, symbolised French culture? The battle by the opponents was expertly led by André Fermigier, an art historian, teacher at the Sorbonne and a formidable columnist at *Le Monde*. He railed against the project in articles which led to a mass of often very virulent reactions. François Mitterrand remained imperturbable, loyal to Pei's idea and deaf to all attacks.

30 May 1989 was a key date in the museum's history, as from the architectural point of view it symbolised the end of one era and the start of another. The building unveiled to the astonished eyes of the guests that day would quickly become the very symbol of the museum: how did a monument which had been so disparaged and caused such a violent controversy manage to become the universal illustration of the museum? A real miracle occurred during the hours which followed the opening of the Napoleon Court, even before the public had entered this surprising area for the first time. The lines and materials used by Pei were so simple, so beautiful and so pure that

In the front row, François Mitterrand, centre, with Jack Lang (Minister for Culture) to his left, and Émile Biasini (President of the government owned body the Grand Louvre) to his right. Pierre Bérégovoy (Prime Minister) in the second row, during the inauguration of the Pyramid.

The Louvre could then launch the biggest operation to expand its exhibition spaces in its long history.

they could not fail to bring together even the most negative detractors in a sense of shared admiration! It was even possible to imagine that André Fermigier, who had died a year earlier, would perhaps have liked the light of the Pyramid and the wonderful views it afforded of the Napoleon III façades which surrounded it. Together with the Napoleon Hall, on the first day the public discovered the remains of the Louvre of Philippe Auguste and Charles V, which had been uncovered a few years earlier and made ready for visitors. Who would have thought that one day they would stroll amongst the foundations of a building which disappeared in the mid-17th century and whose existence had been known only to a few experts?

The March 1989 opening slightly preceded the celebrations of the bicentenary of the Revolution. This event also had a direct effect on the future of the Louvre, as on 15 July Michel Laclotte, the Museum Director, was handed the keys of the Richelieu Wing, abandoned by the Finance Ministry, which had moved to Bercy. The Louvre could then launch the biggest operation to expand its exhibition spaces in its long history. When the new halls opened in 1993, on four levels and around three covered internal courtyards, the surface area of the museum had increased by a third.

The opening of the Pyramid and the launch of the second phase of the Grand Louvre project had a direct and rather unexpected consequence, namely the rapid increase in visitor numbers. The magnificent but fusty pre-1989 museum had welcomed an average of two million visitors a year, but this number would soon reach three, then four million... Almost nine million people pass today through the Napoleon Hall which, more than twenty years after its inauguration, still performs its role as main entrance and welcome for visitors perfectly. It is no doubt this which can gauge the success of the operation launched in 1981: over thirty years, it has adapted to the changes of the new millennium without any problems.

Queue of visitors outside the Pyramid waiting to enter the museum

Architecture
The six main stages of construction

The Library Tower

From a simple 12th century fortress intended to protect Paris, the château transformed into an immense palace, a symbol of the Kings' power once the threat of invasion passed. Over the course of eight centuries, the greatest architects contributed to its glory. After the fall of the monarchy, the Republic and then Napoleon invented the concept of universal museum that would serve as the model for museums around the world.

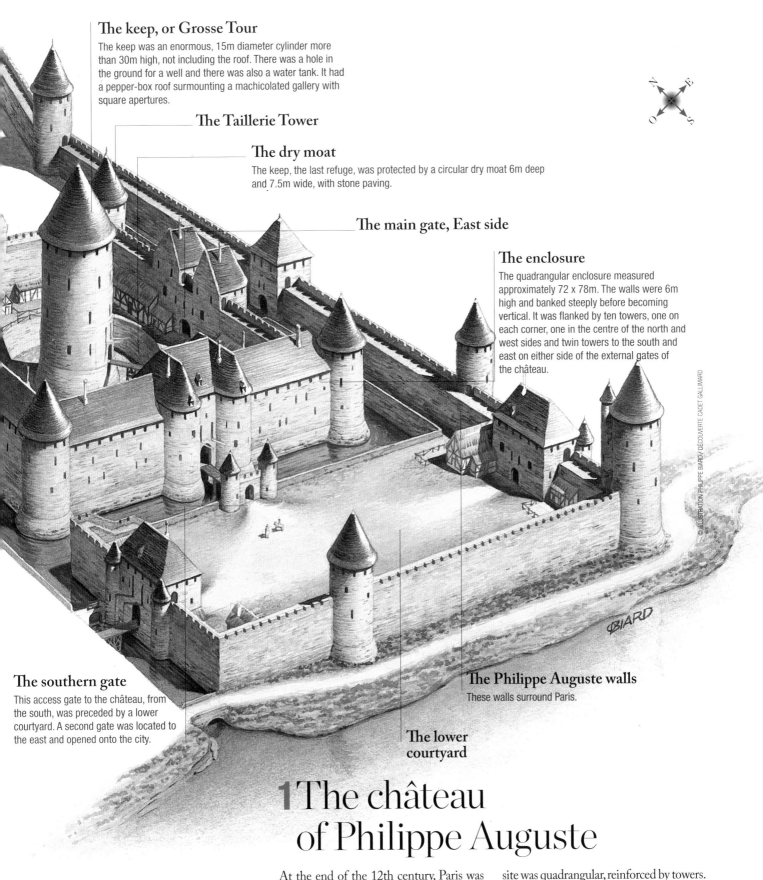

The keep, or Grosse Tour

The keep was an enormous, 15m diameter cylinder more than 30m high, not including the roof. There was a hole in the ground for a well and there was also a water tank. It had a pepper-box roof surmounting a machicolated gallery with square apertures.

The Taillerie Tower

The dry moat

The keep, the last refuge, was protected by a circular dry moat 6m deep and 7.5m wide, with stone paving.

The main gate, East side

The enclosure

The quadrangular enclosure measured approximately 72 x 78m. The walls were 6m high and banked steeply before becoming vertical. It was flanked by ten towers, one on each corner, one in the centre of the north and west sides and twin towers to the south and east on either side of the external gates of the château.

The southern gate

This access gate to the château, from the south, was preceded by a lower courtyard. A second gate was located to the east and opened onto the city.

The Philippe Auguste walls

These walls surround Paris.

The lower courtyard

This drawing is the interpretation of a partially documented historic representation.

1 The château of Philippe Auguste

At the end of the 12th century, Paris was under threat from the English and without real defences. Philippe Auguste thus began the construction of an outer wall to protect the city; he reinforced it by ordering the construction to the west, thus facing the potential enemy, of a château outside the city. The Louvre was born. The site was quadrangular, reinforced by towers. It had two gates, one facing the Seine to the south and the other facing the city to the east. In the centre of the courtyard, the Grosse Tour served as a keep and dominated the entire construction. This first Louvre was not a residence for sovereigns, but just housed a garrison and an arsenal.

©ILLUSTRATION PHILIPPE BIARD / DÉCOUVERTE CADET GALLIMARD

The Keep or Grosse Tour

The Great Staircase

The new staircase designed by Pierre de Montreuil was attached to the north wing. It was helicoidal and double spiral and richly decorated with statues and adornments. It was greatly admired and would be copied throughout the Empire.

The roofs

All the roof coverings were improved and completed so that the Louvre displayed a forest of decorative turrets and chimneys. Adornments embellished the tops of the roofs and contributed to the sumptuous image of the palace.
As there are no remains, it is impossible to confirm that the roofs shown here are historically accurate.
The view of the château under Charles V in the "Very Rich Hours of the Duke of Berry" (see p. 8) inspired all reconstruction attempts.

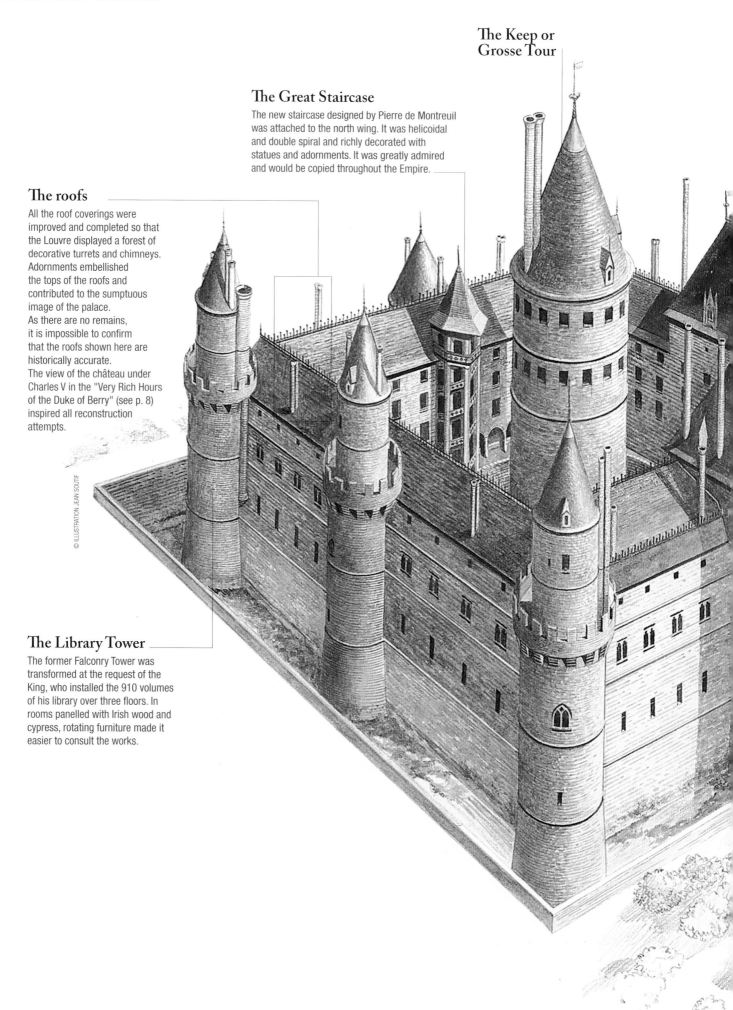

© ILLUSTRATION JEAN SOUTIF

The Library Tower

The former Falconry Tower was transformed at the request of the King, who installed the 910 volumes of his library over three floors. In rooms panelled with Irish wood and cypress, rotating furniture made it easier to consult the works.

Modern dwellings

Pierre de Montreuil constructed two new dwellings and heightened the existing wings. New apertures, which were wide and high, provided the necessary light to the reception rooms and apartments inside.

2 The Medieval Louvre under Charles V

In 1356, during the Hundred Years' War, Étienne Marcel, the Merchant Provost, began the construction of a new city wall intended to protect Paris from English danger. The fortified construction was completed by the newly crowned Charles V. The new wall brought the recent suburbs of the city under its protection. It also included the Louvre of Philippe Auguste, which was now no longer outside the city. The château had now lost its strategic defensive role for ever. In 1360, the King entrusted Pierre de Montreuil with managing the work to modify the nature of the building, which involved constructing new dwellings and remodelling the existing parts. To the north of the Louvre, a garden was adorned with decorative and medicinal plants; to the west vast outhouses were built. In the course of a few years, the sombre fortress became a modern, light and sumptuously decorated palace. The King often stayed there, as did his successor Charles VI. On the latter's death, Paris was occupied by the English. For a century, the Louvre ceased to be the residence of Kings.

The corner tower

The tower was constructed under Philippe Auguste and was the meeting point between the former Paris city walls, of which it marked the end point on the banks of the Seine, and the new walls leading westwards. Its location corresponded to the start of the current Passerelle des Arts.

This drawing is the interpretation of a partially documented historical representation.

3 The Louvre of Henri IV

In 1526, François I decided to live in the capital permanently and chose the Louvre as his residence. Although the Grosse Tour was immediately knocked down and the apartments renovated, it was not until 1546 that the King began the construction of a new wing on the site of the west wing of the medieval Louvre. Pierre Lescot did most of the building work after the accession to the throne of Henri II, who also had a new south wing built, and where the two met, the Pavillon du Roi which dominated the whole construction.

In 1564, Catherine de Medici, Henri II's widow, ordered work to start on the Tuileries to the west. A project was quickly developed to connect the two palaces of the Louvre and the Tuileries by means of a succession of courtyards and buildings and the four-fold increase in the size of the Louvre. It was Henri IV who initiated this major project by building the Grande Galerie along the banks of the Seine. With the exception of the extensions to the Tuileries Palace, the project remained on paper.

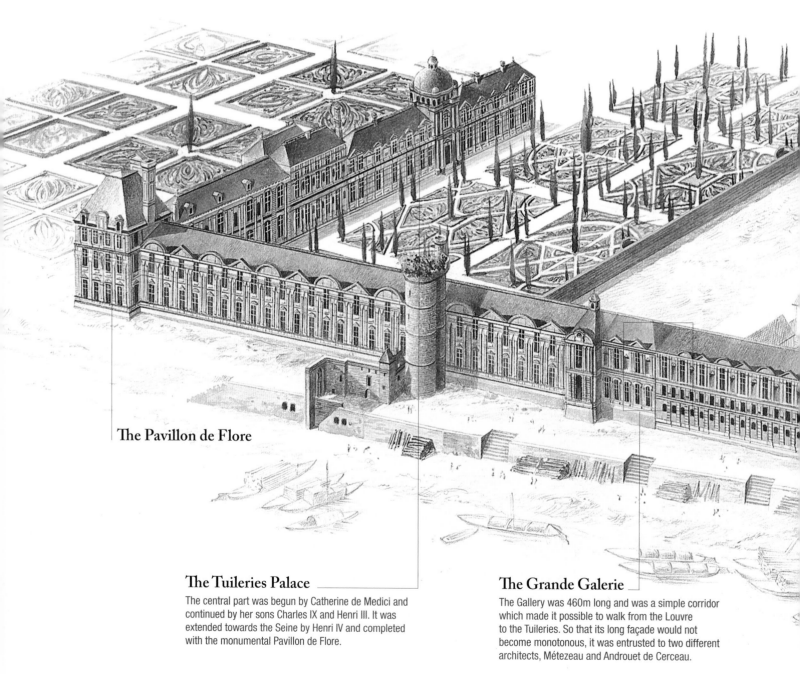

The Pavillon de Flore

The Tuileries Palace

The central part was begun by Catherine de Medici and continued by her sons Charles IX and Henri III. It was extended towards the Seine by Henri IV and completed with the monumental Pavillon de Flore.

The Grande Galerie

The Gallery was 460m long and was a simple corridor which made it possible to walk from the Louvre to the Tuileries. So that its long façade would not become monotonous, it was entrusted to two different architects, Métezeau and Androuet de Cerceau.

The Pavillon du Roi

This was the dominant part of the Louvre during this period. Placed at the junction between the two new wings of the palace, it contained the King's apartments spread over three floors. It was then absorbed into the construction work ordered by Louis XIV.

The west and south wings

These were designed by Pierre Lescot according to the same model. The façades of the Lescot wing (west) were one of the best examples of Renaissance architecture in Paris. The Seine-facing façade of the south wing can no longer be seen.

The remains of the medieval Louvre

The oldest parts of the Louvre were only partially demolished in the early 17th century. The north and south wings still stood and would not disappear for another fifty years.

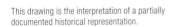

This drawing is the interpretation of a partially documented historical representation.

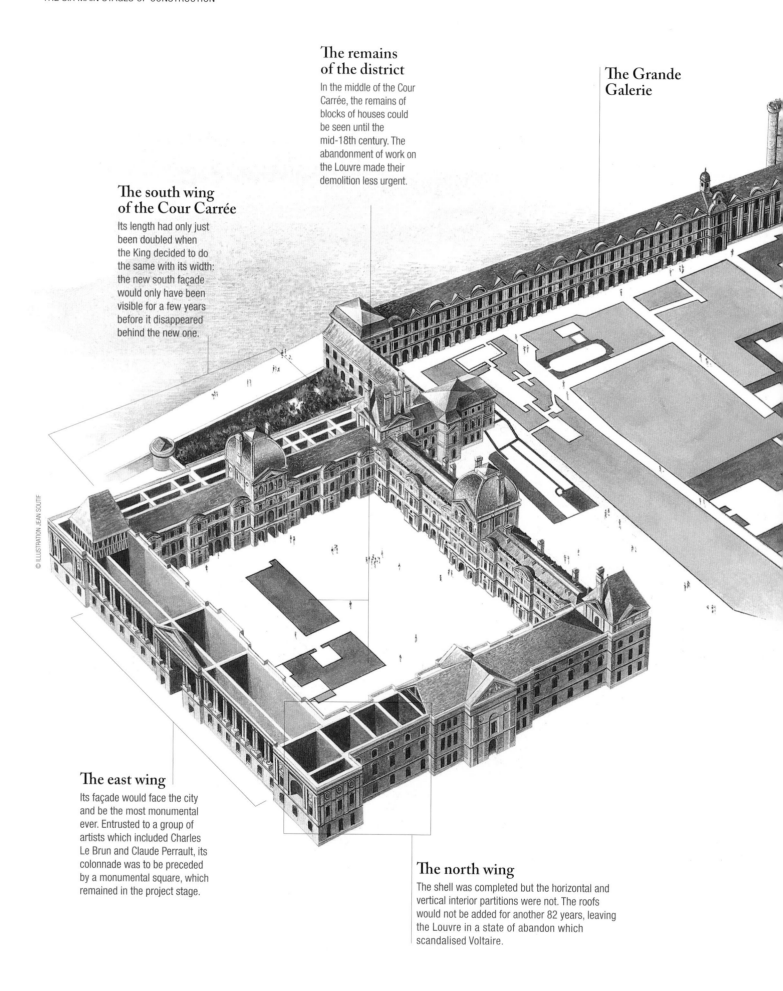

The remains of the district

In the middle of the Cour Carrée, the remains of blocks of houses could be seen until the mid-18th century. The abandonment of work on the Louvre made their demolition less urgent.

The Grande Galerie

The south wing of the Cour Carrée

Its length had only just been doubled when the King decided to do the same with its width: the new south façade would only have been visible for a few years before it disappeared behind the new one.

The east wing

Its façade would face the city and be the most monumental ever. Entrusted to a group of artists which included Charles Le Brun and Claude Perrault, its colonnade was to be preceded by a monumental square, which remained in the project stage.

The north wing

The shell was completed but the horizontal and vertical interior partitions were not. The roofs would not be added for another 82 years, leaving the Louvre in a state of abandon which scandalised Voltaire.

© ILLUSTRATION JEAN SOUTIF

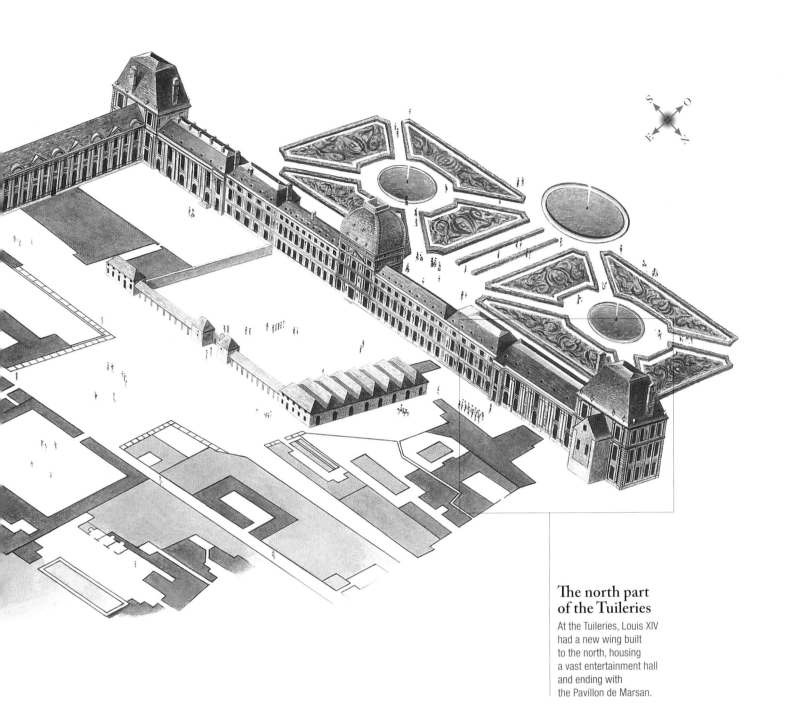

The north part of the Tuileries

At the Tuileries, Louis XIV had a new wing built to the north, housing a vast entertainment hall and ending with the Pavillon de Marsan.

4 The Louvre of Louis XIV

When he came to the throne on 1643, the young king inherited a palace which resembled a vast building site. Located in the heart of a densely built-up district, the Louvre was a collection of buildings whose oldest parts dated back to the early 13th century and whose most recent were unfinished. The King's took action in two areas. The first was the Cour Carrée, which Louis XIV wanted to complete.

The Galerie d'Apollon which replaced the Galerie des Rois which had burnt down, marked the start of his action. The King then ordered the construction of new wings to the north and east of the future Cour Carrée. By doing this, he doubled the length of the south wing in order to close off the space. The western façade, facing the city, was more problematic and in 1664 the King summoned

the Italian Le Bernin, whose ideas seduced but did not convince. The construction of a new façade was finally entrusted to a group of artists which included Claude Perrault. The second area of work was a consequence of the first: as the Louvre was then uninhabitable, Louis XIV had the Tuileries finished so that he could live there temporarily. He would not return to the Louvre.

This drawing is the interpretation of a partially documented historical representation.

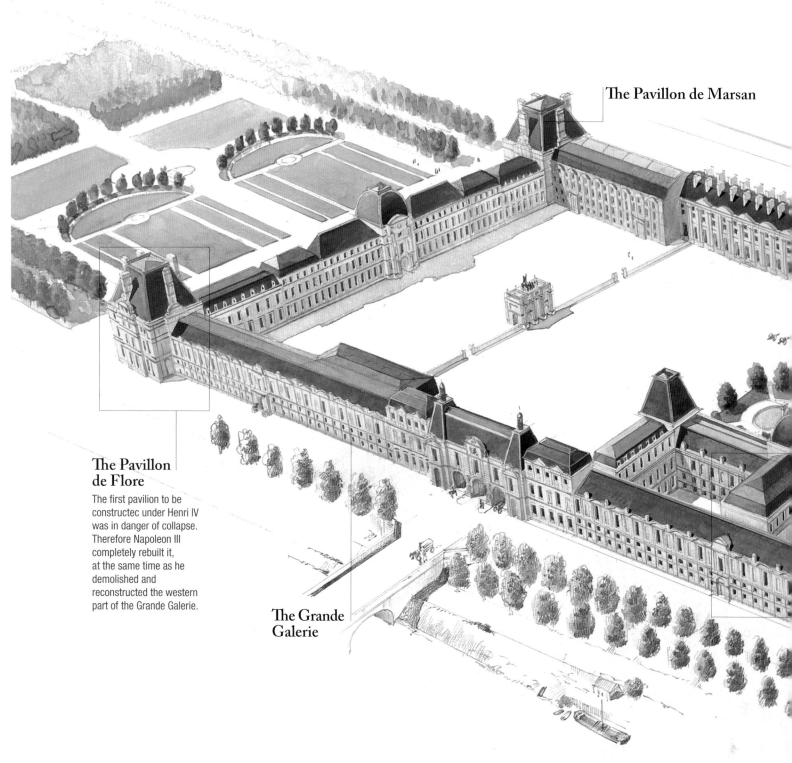

The Pavillon de Marsan

The Pavillon de Flore

The first pavilion to be constructec under Henri IV was in danger of collapse. Therefore Napoleon III completely rebuilt it, at the same time as he demolished and reconstructed the western part of the Grande Galerie.

The Grande Galerie

5 The Louvre of Napoleon III

Napoleon III began his construction work in 1852 with the demolition of the last remains of the district located between the Louvre and the Tuileries. In their place were constructed the main bodies of two large buildings which formed the boundary of the vast Napoleon Court. Their architecture was inspired by

that of the Renaissance Louvre, whose decorative elements it copied. The sizes of the new pavilions were taken from the Pavillon Lemercier or the Central Pavilion of the Tuileries.

Once the new Court was completed, the Emperor ordered the demolition of the western part of the Grande Galerie,

which was badly damaged, and replaced it with a new wing. Doubling the width of the Tuileries Palace would complete the redevelopment of the imperial complex, but the war of 1870 interrupted the work and the destruction wreaked by the Commune threatened the very survival of the largest building in the city.

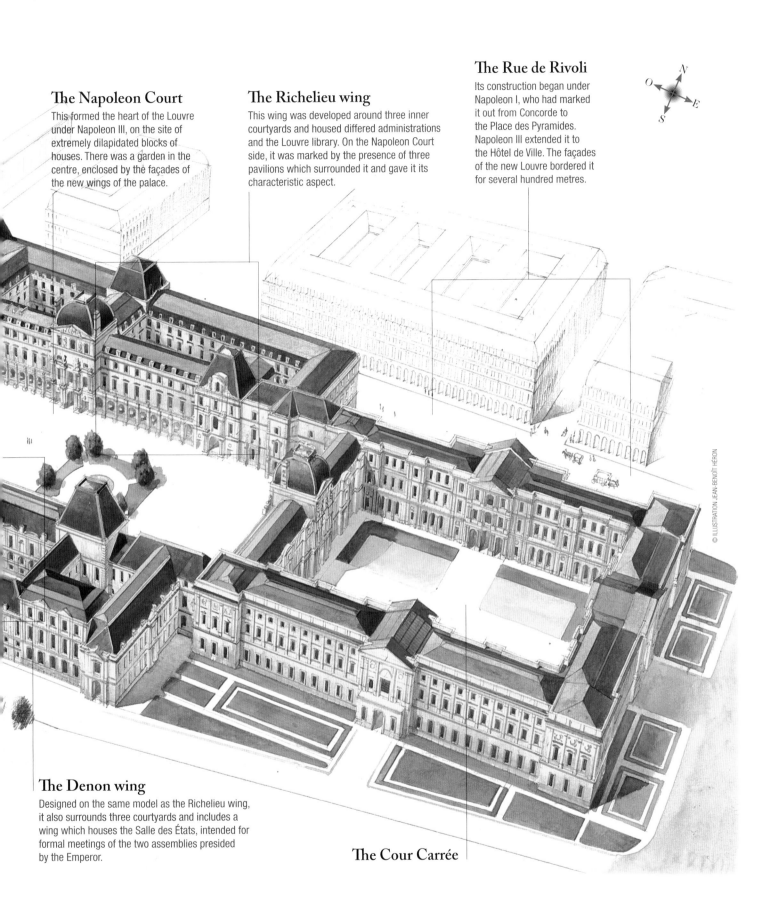

The Napoleon Court

This formed the heart of the Louvre under Napoleon III, on the site of extremely dilapidated blocks of houses. There was a garden in the centre, enclosed by the façades of the new wings of the palace.

The Richelieu wing

This wing was developed around three inner courtyards and housed differed administrations and the Louvre library. On the Napoleon Court side, it was marked by the presence of three pavilions which surrounded it and gave it its characteristic aspect.

The Rue de Rivoli

Its construction began under Napoleon I, who had marked it out from Concorde to the Place des Pyramides. Napoleon III extended it to the Hôtel de Ville. The façades of the new Louvre bordered it for several hundred metres.

The Denon wing

Designed on the same model as the Richelieu wing, it also surrounds three courtyards and includes a wing which houses the Salle des États, intended for formal meetings of the two assemblies presided by the Emperor.

The Cour Carrée

This drawing is the interpretation of a partially documented historical representation.

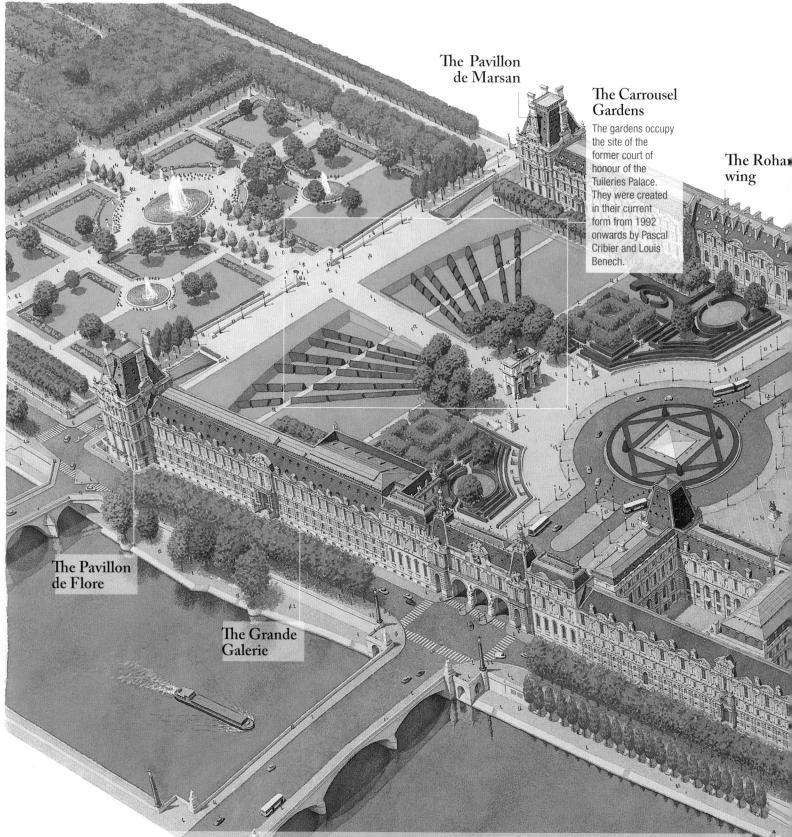

The Pavillon
de Marsan

The Carrousel
Gardens

The gardens occupy
the site of the
former court of
honour of the
Tuileries Palace.
They were created
in their current
form from 1992
onwards by Pascal
Cribier and Louis
Benech.

The Roha
wing

The Pavillon
de Flore

The Grande
Galerie

6 The Louvre in 2000

In May 1871, the Tuileries Palace was burnt down during the Commune. The ruins were demolished twelve years later, opening up the internal area of the Louvre towards the Tuileries Gardens and the major axis to the west of Paris. The Flore and Marsan Pavilions had been burned down but were rebuilt and the Third Republic even planned to complete the Rohan wing, before quickly abandoning the work. Architecturally, the Louvre lay dormant for a century. The Grand Louvre project redesigned the entire complex: the central square of the Napoleon Court was dug up and its basement provided additional space for the museum, surmounted by the Pyramid designed by the architect Ieoh Ming Pei. Further towards the west, a new roundabout controlled the movement of people. Its central platform hid an inverted pyramid which lit up the heart of a new commercial gallery. The redesigned Carrousel gardens opened onto a new terrace on the site of the Tuileries. All the façades of the palace have been restored since 1984.

The Pyramid

The geometrically perfect form of the pyramid was added to the museum's central reception hall, adding light and space. The glass sides and their metallic structure mean that the façades of the Louvre can be seen through them.

The cover of the courtyards of the Richelieu wing

(From left to right, Marly, Puget and Khorsabad)

To allow the display of monumental works, the courtyards of the Richelieu wing were covered with elegant glass roofs designed by Pei. The 1993 opening of the Richelieu wing gave the Louvre a 30% increase in its surface area for the presentation of permanent collections.

The Colonnade moats

The moats were dug at the request of André Malraux in 1964, inspired by known developments in different buildings of this era. No traces remain of this type of project in this location in the time of Louis XIV.

The Cour Carrée

The Visconti court

Previously inaccessible to the public, it was chosen to house the new halls of the Department of Islamic arts. The halls were located on one underground floor and one ground floor; in 2012 they were covered with a golden veil.

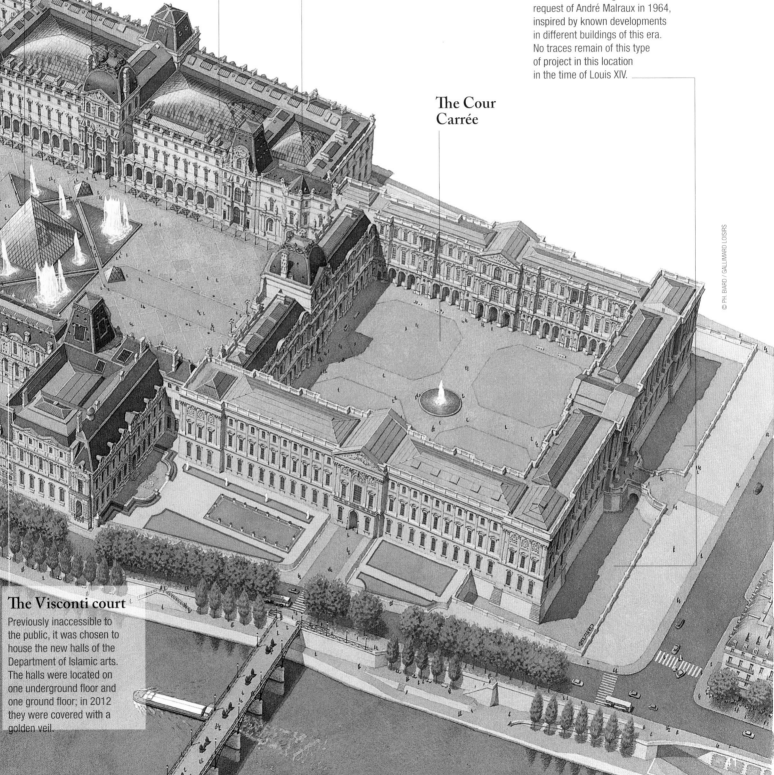

Three façades that represent an era

 The Cour Carrée

The western façade of the Cour Carrée, constructed between 1546 and 1555, is the oldest part of the Louvre visible from the outside.
It was built by Pierre Lescot and adorned with sculptures by Jean Goujon and is one of the jewels of Parisian Renaissance architecture.

String courses

The decor on the cornices which separate the first floor from the attic (mezzanine) above, is a garland of foliage "peopled" with small cupids represented in different positions. The H of Henri II can be seen, in keeping with a common custom at the time which can be found throughout the Louvre.

Initials

The three west-works are surmounted by arched pediments adorned with allegorical figures.
Those on the central west-work are supporting a coat of arms on which is inscribed the initial (H) of Henri II, who completed the construction.
The richness of the decors sculpted by Jean Goujon is representative of French Renaissance taste.

Windows

The windows surroundings are richly decorated, surmounted by a pediment supported by decorative scrolls. They are inspired by ancient models copied by 15th century Italian architects. The mythical, grimacing masks of the pediments were inspired by Roman motifs propagated by engravings.

Decor

The attic is extremely richly decorated.
It aligns great allegorical figures placed at
the top of the west works and representations
of chained prisoners or military trophies.
Once again, the inspiration for the decor comes
from ancient times, particularly in the series of
arms and armour.

Levels

The elevation of the Lescot façade shows the
superimposition of three levels clearly separated
by projecting cornices. They run along the whole
length of the façade and accentuate its impression
of width. Isolated in a courtyard which was then
four times smaller than it is now, this device gave
the building a greater presence.

Orders

On the two lower levels of the façade, columns
or engaged pilasters delimit each bay, inspired
by the great Roman monuments of Antiquity,
such as the Coliseum and the Marcellus theatre,
and the first Renaissance-style Italian palaces
built in Florence and Rome in the 15th century.

Portico

Against the ground floor façade, Lescot placed
a portico consisting of three arches within which
windows opened. These were the façades
of monuments from the Roman period, civic
basilicas, circuses, theatres and amphitheatres,
which no doubt served as models.

Niches

The niches adorning
the two lower levels
of the three west
works were originally
intended to house
sculptures. As this part
of the decor remained
unfinished, copies of
ancient works were
placed there in the
19th century. These
works were slightly
too small and of fairly
average quality
compared with the
work of Goujon.

The Seine Side

Constructed by Le Vau, the large, Seine-facing façade is without doubt one of the best examples of the Classical style from the time of the reign of Louis XIV.

Initials

Louis XIV built this part of the Louvre. In the upper parts of the façade, large medallions bordered by garlands of foliage enclose the double L of the King's initials. Most of the royal initials on the façades were removed during the Revolution and re-engraved under the Restoration.

Levels

The elevation of the façade designed by Le Vau shows a clear separation between three levels: a solid crepidoma, a very high piano nobile and a second, lower, level, which is actually a mezzanine. It is all crowned by a balustrade which hides the almost flat roofs.

Mascarons

Mascarons decorated with heads of people or animals could be found frequently in the 17th and 18th centuries. Each one was different and they sometimes depicted monsters or hybrid beings inspired by mythological texts. Those on the windows of the crepidoma are some of the rare sculptured decors on the façade.

Capitals

The choice of the Corinthian order to adorn the façade is an important element in the definition of French Classicism. Highly prized by Ancient Romans, the Corinthian is the most monumental and most decorative of architectural styles; it lends solemnity and sumptuousness to the monument.

Roofs

As was often the case in the time of Louis XIV, the roofs are invisible. They are almost flat and are hidden behind the stone balustrade. In earlier periods, until Louis XIII, roofs remained visible and played an important role in the general structure of buildings.

Balustrade

A monumental balustrade crowns the façade. It surmounts a projecting cornice which tops the monument and rests on the Corinthian capitals of the pilasters. The use of high balustrades is typical of French Classicism. It was also found later at Versailles.

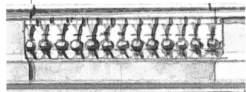

Orders

The architects of the Sun King brought together the two upper levels of the façade by the use of a colossal order composed of majestic pilasters with a Corinthian capital. The use of the colossal order is characteristic of the Baroque period in Europe and of Classicism in France (17th and 18th centuries).

Piano nobile

The presence of a piano nobile indicates the predominance given to first floor rooms in comparison with those on the second floor. In royal buildings, it was there that could be found the salons and the rooms of the residence, which required a much greater ceiling height.

Cornice

The frieze with its vegetation motif which crowned the crepidoma is the only notable decorative element of the façade, as the sculptures on the large central pediment were not added until the 19th century. The completeness of the decor and the domination of the architectural lines are key elements of Louis XIV architecture.

Crepidoma

The crepidoma plays an important role in the south façade of the Louvre. On the cornice which surmounts it is the colossal order which joins the floors. Relatively large and with apertures which seem smaller than they are in reality, it has no decor other than the masks which surmount the windows.

The Pavillon Colbert

Designed by Visconti but created by Lefuel, the Pavillon Colbert is representative of Napoleon III-era constructions within the Louvre Palace. The adopted style is widely inspired by Renaissance constructions of the late 16th and early 17th centuries, in particular the Lescot and Lemercier wings.

Pediment

The enormous crown which surmounts the central bay is characterised by an overabundance of decorative elements. Statues and reliefs are inspired by the decorations of older façades, but differ in their dimensions and complexity. The Napoleon III style often used a very popular sculpted decor.

Decor

The large number of decorative elements defines the style of the Second Empire. The bosses which reinforce the corners of the pavilion were an ancient tradition frequently found during the Renaissance. With no other function than decoration, here they weigh down the decorative structure of the construction.

Windows

The frames of the main floor windows were decorated with simple pediments of a very classical design, resting on consoles; they copy models created under Louis XIV for the apertures in the city- and Seine-facing façades of the Cour Carrée.

Caryatids

To frame the large aperture formed by the pavilion crown, Lefuel had large caryatids created, which were copies of those sculpted by Sarazin two and a half centuries earlier for the Pavillon Sully. They were heavier and did not have the grace of the works which inspired them.

Motifs

The six pavilions which form the Richelieu and Denon wings reproduce an architectural motif inaugurated by Henri II in the Pavillon du Roi of the Cour Carrée. The architects of Napoleon III supplemented them with a rich sculptured decor whose sumptuousness characterises the style of the era.

Model

The mezzanine formed by the upper level of the pavilion repeats exactly the decorative principle of the higher parts of the Lescot wing: the windows are framed by decorative reliefs showing military trophies. Placed in the upper part of the façade, they are part of the overabundance of the crowns.

Allegories

Like Goujon in the Lescot wing in the mid-16th century, Lefuel framed the main upstairs window and the circular ground-floor apertures with allegorical figures which seem to rest on the frames. Very little of the surface area of the façade is left without decoration.

Inspiration

The juxtaposition of architectural and decorative items from different eras characterises every wing of the Louvre constructed or restored during the time of Napoleon III. This practice allowed Visconti and Lefuel to easily integrate their new creations into the heart of the pre-existing building.

Orders

To accentuate the central bay of the construction, on two levels Lefuel framed it with pairs of columns with Corinthian capitals. These create an important projection in relation to the line of the wall, giving more dramatic effects of light and shade and accentuating the visual presence of the pavilion.

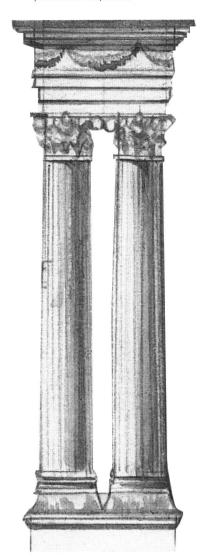

A history of art
illustrated by 140 masterpieces

Leonardo da Vinci (1452-1519)
The Monna Lisa [detail]
Circa 1503-1506, oil on poplar wood, 77 x 53 cm.

Antiquity

A long period ranging from the end of the Neolithic age to the early Middle Ages, Antiquity is the first stage in our history of art. During these four thousand years, powerful cities, kingdoms and empires sprang up all around the Mediterranean and the Near East, leading to the emergence of new art forms and practices: the tombs and pyramids in Egypt, classical sculpture in Greece and monumental architecture in Rome are a few well-known examples. The ancient forms and practices had a major influence on the artists and producers of the following centuries, to the point where they became real "models" for them to follow.

Aphrodite, **called** *Venus de Milo* [detail]
Circa 100 B.C., Melos, Greece, marble, H. 211 cm.

The Ancient East

While agriculture and writing were developing between the 8th and 3rd millennium B.C., in the Ancient East, vast urban systems were emerging that would soon give rise to powerful empires. Artistic creation accompanied these upheavals by enshrining the new hierarchies that were established in these developing societies. The figure of the leader, the king, the sovereign took the leading role in an extraordinarily diverse world.

▼ 1 *Statue of a human figure*
The Levant (excavation at 'Ain Ghazal, Jordan), 7th millennium B.C.,
gypsum plaster, eyelids and pupils made of bitumen, H. 105 cm.

This hand-modelled plaster statue is the oldest work preserved by the Louvre Museum. It dates back to the pre-ceramic Neolithic era, during which the farming communities of the Ancient East became sedentary and organised. Art accompanied these transformations by underlining and enshrining the new hierarchies of these budding societies: this effigy probably represents a clan leader and would have played an important role in ritual ceremonies.

▶ 2 *Ebih-Il nu-banda*
Mesopotamia (Mari, Ishtar temple), circa 2350-2250 B.C.,
alabaster, lapis lazuli, shell, bitumen, 53 x 21 x 37 cm.

Found during excavations directed by André Parrot in Syria from 1933 onwards.

The figure of the leader became one of the major subjects of artistic creation in the city-states that made up Mesopotamia. The great refinement and special care taken over the effigy of Ebih-Il, dignitary of the kingdom of Mari, show how great his power was within the community. The statuette, an offering to the goddess of Love and War, Ishtar, also shows the devotion of the figure, who sits with his hands joined, smiling confidently at the deity he is praying to.

◀ 3 *Gudea, Prince of Lagash, statue with "overflowing vase", dedicated to the goddess Geshtinanna*
Mesopotamia (Tello, formerly Girsu), circa 2120 B.C., dolerite, 62 x 25.6 cm.

Gudea, Prince of Lagash, took great care over his image: as a ruler and builder, he had sculptures of himself placed in the main temples of the city. The sculptures of him played a political role: they attributed remarkable qualities to the leader while establishing him as a central figure of the urban system he governed. In fact they carried a message: here the overflowing vase is a fertility symbol. Gudea therefore appears as a ruler who guarantees prosperity for his subjects.

▲ 4 *Code of Hammurabi,*
King of Babylon
Mesopotamia, 1792-1750 B.C.,
basalt, 225 x 65 cm.

Unearthed during excavations led by Jacques de Morgan in 1901-1902 in Susa.

The King's words alone organised, governed and directed life in the City. They dictated the laws and dispensed justice. Hammurabi, King of Babylon, is shown here at the top of a basalt stele, bearing one of the most comprehensive codes of justice in Antiquity: erected at the very centre of the city, the aim of this monument was to enshrine the sovereign word while reminding people of its divine origin. The god of Sun and Justice, Shamash, gives the King the power to govern his subjects here.

◀ **5 et 6** *Bulls with human heads and wings, from the palace of Sargon II*
Mesopotamia (Khorsabad, Assyria), 713-706 B.C., gypsum alabaster, 420 x 436 x 97 cm.

Unearthed during excavations carried out from 1843 to 1854 by the French consul in Mosul, Paul Émile Botta.

The external attributes of royal power gave the human government a direct relationship with the gods. These two winged bulls with human heads, which guarded the doors of the palace of Sargon II, King of Assyria, offered divine protection against any enemies. At the same time, they formed a sacred enclosure around the sovereign, enshrining him as the "curate and high priest of the god Assur". Immobile when viewed from the front, in motion when seen in profile, these magical creatures are typical of Assyrian sculpture, which was both realistic and highly stylised.

▶ **7** *Capital of a column in the audience hall (apadana) in the palace of Darius I*
Ancient Iran (Susa), circa 510 B.C., limestone, H. 760 cm.

Reconstituted from fragments found during excavations at the Susa palace by Marcel Dieulafoy in 1885-1886.

This colossal capital stood on top of one of the thirty-six columns in the throne room in the palace of Darius I, the Great King of Persia, in Susa. At this seat of power, symbolism played an essential role: the bull, an expression of strength and power, is also a key figure in Persian mythology. It is also an old Mesopotamian motif, combined here with Egyptian, Greek and Persian elements. The capital is a mixture of styles and influences, providing proof of the recent unification of the various parts of the Empire.

◀ **8** *Archer frieze*

Ancient Iran (Susa), circa 510 B.C., glazed silica bricks,
475 x 375 cm (each brick: 8.5 x 33 x 17 cm).

A real army provided protection for Darius I in Susa: thousands of archers made of glazed bricks lined the walls surrounding the palace. While they show the richness and strength of a stable Empire, we do not yet know everything about this depiction. Are they "Immortals", elite guards devoted to the Great King in body and soul, or do they represent the whole Persian population, recently unified, gathering around its sovereign?

▼ **9** *Vase in the shape of a winged ibex*

Ancient Iran, 539-333 B.C., silver and gold, 27 x 15 x 10 cm.

Very early on, cultural exchanges influenced artistic creation: various Greek, Persian and Egyptian mythologies co-existed and were interconnected. This vase handle illustrates this hybridisation and displays a mixture of influences. The winged ibex, a magical creature from the eastern pantheon, rests its hind legs on a mask of Silenus, a Greek figure linked to the cult of Dionysos. The latter appears in Persia in the form of Bes, an Egyptian deity similar to Silenus.

▼ **10** *Divine triad*

The Levant (Palmyra, Syria), 1st half of the 1st century A.D.,
limestone, 69 x 56 cm.

The Ancient East was profoundly shaped by hybrid forms and a mixture of influences, as was the case with Palmyra, a cosmopolitan city and centre of a major trade network, where this sculpture comes from. The supreme god Baalshamin, in the middle; the Moon god Aglibôl, left; and the Sun god Malakbêl, right, are dressed in the Roman style, with a tunic and belted armour. However, the hairstyle, beard and trousers of the supreme god are in the Iranian style, as proof of the diversity of exchanges throughout the region.

Egypt

For around three-thousand years, Egyptian art remained remarkably consistent, in terms of its forms as well as its purpose - to give eternal life to the things it represented. Writing, architecture, sculpture and soon painting would thus provide a kind of transition between the worlds of the living and the dead, by keeping the image or name of the person depicted alive forever.

▶ 11 *Scribe sitting cross-legged*

Saqqara, Old Empire (4th dynasty), circa 2620-2500 B.C., limestone, rock crystal, magnesite, copper with arsenic, wood, 53 x 44 x 35 cm.

Discovered by Auguste Mariette in 1850 in a sacked cemetery, and given to the Louvre by the Egyptian government as a shared archaeological find.

In Ancient Egypt, the scribe was the man who could read and write. He became the central figure of the vast administrative system built up by this civilisation, which is still famous for its remarkable mastery of writing. Nothing is known about the man represented here, but the exceptional quality of the statue shows that he was high-ranking. He was certainly a high dignitary who was active during the time of the great pyramids.

◀ 12 *Stele of the Serpent King*

Abydos, 1st dynasty, circa 3000 B.C., limestone, 143 x 65 x 25 cm.

This funerary stele from the 3rd millennium B.C. bears one of the oldest known hieroglyphs: it is inscribed with the name of the sovereign whose tomb it adorns, Horus Djed, the "Serpent King". Egyptian art is an art of eternity. Inscriptions like this one were designed to ensure the deceased would survive in the earthly world and the afterlife. The Egyptians believed that sacred writing had the magical power of preserving an immortal "double" of the person it referred to.

▶ 13 *Tamutnefret's coffins*

21th dynasty, 1295-1186 B.C., coated, painted and gilded wood, the largest measuring 192 x 59 x 43 cm.

The cult of the dead was very important to Egyptians, who sought to stop their body from disappearing forever. The mummy preserved the body and was placed in several coffins carved with the image of the deceased. These were decorated with texts and figures with magical properties, providing protection and a container for the soul. The patterns painted on the coffin also convey an idealised view of the dead person's life, as is the case here for Tamutnefret, a great lady from the 11th dynasty.

▶ **14** *Mastaba of Akhethetep* [detail]
Saqqara, 5th dynasty, 2400 B.C., painted limestone, low relief.

Bought by the Louvre in 1903 from the Egyptian authorities, who sold antiques to ensure they would be preserved by great institutions.

A mastaba is a trapezoid funerary monument erected on top of the mortuary chamber where the deceased lay, connected to it by a well that was filled in after the burial. The walls of this chapel are adorned with sculpted images that accompanied the dead person on their last journey. In Egyptian art, it was believed that representations had the power to make their subjects real and immortal. Here, the pleasure of music is given to Akhethetep, dignitary of the Old Empire, for all eternity.

▶ **15** *The Great Sphinx of Tanis*
Tanis, Old Empire (18th dynasty), circa 2600 B.C., granite, 183 x 480 x 154 cm.

Discovered in 1825 in the ruins of the temple of Amon-Re in Tanis, then acquired by King Charles X for his private collection.

The Egyptian sphinx gives the sovereign the body of a lion, the earthly incarnation of the Sun god. It establishes the greatness and power of a figure at one with the divine. The sculpture then becomes the living image of the King, who is assured of his own eternal life: the sphinx is in fact the immortal guardian of sacred places, first and foremost the royal necropolis, which it protects forever against the enemies of Egypt. It will forever remain as the symbol of the strength and power of a pharaoh, whose identity here is unknown to us.

▶ **16** *Amenophis IV-Akhenaton*
Karnak, New Empire (18th dynasty), 1353-1337 B.C., sandstone, 137 x 88 x 60 cm.

Given to France by the Egyptian government in 1972 to thank it for its help with saving the monuments of Nubia.

The representation of the King changed drastically during the reign of Amenophis IV, better known as Akhenaton. The pharaoh, who initiated a dual theological and artistic revolution, imposed new aesthetic canons for the royal image, as shown by this colossal statue of him, a fragment of a column at Aton temple in Karnak. The long face, narrow features, full lips and chin exaggerated by a disproportionate false beard became typical features of a form of royal statuary which was caricatured, excessive and often androgynous.

◄ 17 *The Goddess Hathor and King Seti I*

Thebes, New Empire (19th dynasty), 1290-1179 B.C., painted limestone, 226 x 105 cm.

Taken by Champollion from Seti's tomb in the Valley of Kings and bought by the Louvre in 1829.

The upheavals that took place during the reign of Akhenaton did not detract from the extraordinary permanence of the artistic forms and conventions that shaped Ancient Egypt throughout its history. For example, in this low relief from the royal tomb of Seti I, the characters are always depicted from different angles: the pelvis and head are seen in profile while the eye and shoulders face forward. This aesthetic canon is closely associated with the idea of eternity, as shown by this scene, where the goddess Hathor welcomes the deceased sovereign to the world of the dead.

▲ **19** *Christ and Abbot Mena*

Bawit, 7th-8th century A.D., sycamore fig tree wood, 57 x 57 cm.

Discovered in 1900 by Jean Clédat and given to the Louvre by the Egyptian government in 1901-1902 as a shared archaeological find.

The Christianisation of Egypt, from the 4th century A.D., did not disrupt the rise of painting in this region, as proven by this remarkable icon discovered at Bawit monastery, where it probably adorned one of the churches. The absolute frontality of the figures of Christ, right, and Abbot Mena, the head of the monastery, left, are reminiscent of the fixed depictions of Ancient Egypt. The expressiveness of their gazes, on the other hand, shows the influence of the Fayoum portraits and the diversity that characterised Egyptian art in late Antiquity.

▲ **18** *Portrait of a woman, said to be "from Fayoum"*

Thebes, circa 161-180 B.C., encaustic painting on wood, 33 x 20 cm.

The artistic work produced during Antiquity also included painting. The oldest portraits painted on wood in fact date back to the first centuries of our era and were discovered in Egypt, in the Fayoum region. This technique was introduced by the Romans, who combined their own traditions with the Egyptian mummification rite: they placed a portrait of the deceased, painted while they were alive, on top of the mummy, leaving behind a final image of them which was both highly idealised and very expressive.

Greece

The art of Ancient Greek civilisation was guided by the search for formal perfection and an ideal beauty that was expressed fully during the so-called "classical" period, in the 5th century B.C. Representations of humans gradually became more animated and gained a sense of movement that breathed life into them. In the 3rd century B.C., during the "Hellenistic" period, this movement would display renewed sensuality and expressivity.

▼ *20 Head of a female statue of the "idol with crossed arms" type*
Cyclades, 2700-2300 B.C., marble, H. 27 cm.
Given to the Louvre in 1873 by Olivier Rayet, who led the excavations in Greece.

In the 3rd millennium B.C., the Cyclades islands were a major centre for artistic activity, best symbolised by its marble "idols". This head probably belonged to one of these nude figurines, standing with their legs joined and their arms folded over their chests. These are these oldest sculpted images of the Greek world. We know little about what these statues meant, but the search for clean lines and geometric simplicity displayed by these statues would have a profound effect on sculpture in the following centuries.

▶ *21 Statue of a woman,*
called the *"Lady of Auxerre"*
Crete, circa 640-630 B.C., limestone,
H. 75 cm (with base).

Bought in 1895 by the caretaker of Auxerre Theatre, then deposited at the municipal museum, this statue was spotted in the reserves by Maxime Collignon in 1907. Two years later, this professor of Greek archaeology at the Sorbonne gave it to the Louvre, which in return gave Auxerre Museum a picture by Harpignies from the collections of the Museum of Luxembourg.

In the 7th century B.C., art was enriched by contributions from the East, as shown by this female statue with an Egyptian hairstyle. Probably made in Crete, it is typical of the time when Greek artists concentrated almost exclusively on representing the human figure, giving the volumes and modelling a realistic treatment. While the model is still very static, showing the legacy of Egyptian representations, it foreshadowed what Greek statuary would become in its search for accurate proportions.

▼ 22 *Head of a horseman,* called the *"Rampin Horseman"*

Athens, circa 550 B.C., marble, H. (head): 27 cm.

Georges Rampin, secretary of the French embassy in St. Petersburg, acquired this work unearthed in 1877 and bequeathed it to the Louvre in 1896.

In around 500 B.C., figures started to be more animated and modelling became for realistic. This victorious horseman, perhaps an Athenian nobleman, hero or demigod, is one of the first examples of movement in Greek sculpture: his head is slightly turned to the left, and he smiles at the spectator. This is one of the oldest equestrian statues in western art; it signals the gradual abandonment of archaic representations while heralding the coming revolution, that of movement.

▶ *Male torso,* called *Torso of Miletus*

Miletus, circa 480-470 B.C., marble, H. 132 cm.

Discovered in 1872 at the Miletus Theatre. Edmond and Gustave de Rothschild, who financed these excavations, gave the sculpture to the Louvre in 1873.

This male torso from the 5th century B.C. still has a certain hieratism specific to earlier archaic figures, but already anticipates innovations that would change the shape of sculpture in the years to come: slightly swaying hips, bulging muscles and robust shoulders give it a great sense of virile power and attach it to the aesthetic canon of the nude athlete, which profoundly influenced all classical statuary.

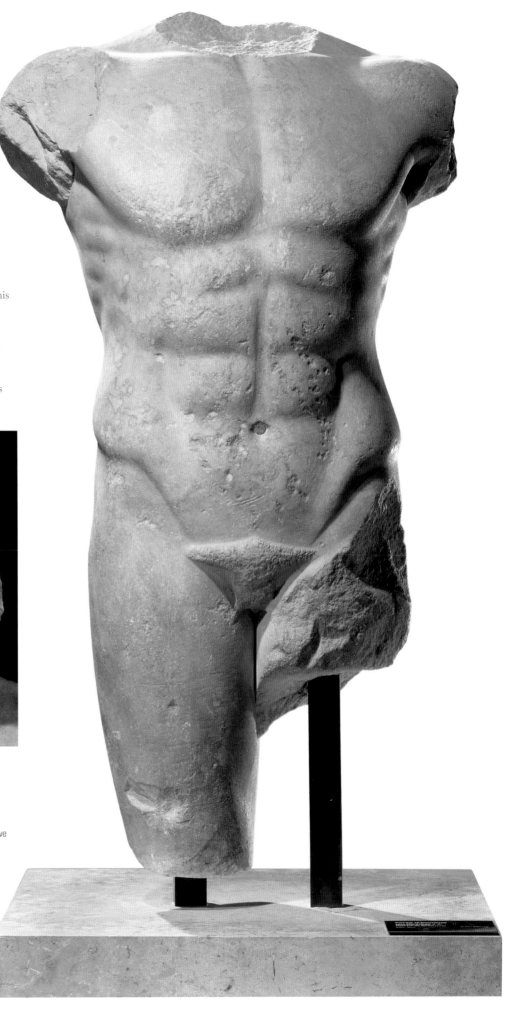

◄ **24 Euphronios** (in Athens from 520 to 470 B.C.)
Attic red figure calyx krater, **called the** *Krater of Antaeus*

Athens, circa 515-510 B.C., H. 44.8 cm, diam. 55 cm.

Early research into movement in Greek art was not carried out by sculptors but by Athenian painters, who liked to animate their depictions. The most famous of these was undoubtedly Euphronios, who painted a vase with this scene showing the demigod Heracles, left, in combat with the giant Antaeus, right, who is about to admit defeat. The dynamic feel given to the painting, and the attention paid to the bulging muscles, powerful anatomy and bodily tension herald the perfect realism of 5th-century sculpture.

▼ **25** *Fragment of a plaque from the eastern frieze of the Parthenon,* **called the** *Plaque of the Ergastines*

Athens, between 445 and 438 B.C., marble, 96 x 207 x 12 cm.

Discovered in 1789, this plaque was seized during the Revolution along with the other property of the Count de Choiseul-Gouffier, French ambassador to the Ottoman Empire. It was given to the Louvre in 1798.

This plaque was part of the long frieze that ran just above the Parthenon colonnade in Athens, all around the building. It depicts the procession of young girls that took place every year to mark the Grand Panathenaia, a ritual festival in Athena's honour. This masterpiece of classic art breaks away from the archaic conventions that dominated sculpture up to that point. It plays with a variety of poses and attitudes to breathe ultimate life and movement into the representation of the body.

▶26 *Aphrodite,*
called *Venus of Milo*

Melos, circa 100 B.C., marble, H. 211 cm.

This statue was unearthed in 1820 by a peasant
in a field on the island of Milo in the Cyclades
archipelago. The Marquis de Rivière (1765-1828),
French ambassador in Constantinople, bought the
sculpture and arranged for it to be transferred to
France with the Turkish authorities in 1821, to
give it to Louis XVIII, who had it put in the Louvre.

The perfect mastery of the spiral
movement which characterises this
remarkable statue of Aphrodite,
goddess of Love, invites us to walk
around it. It marks the high point
of Greek statuary, whose anatomical
studies had now paid off. The
inscrutable face is still reminiscent
of the depictions of previous
centuries, while the way the drape
slides over the hips, loosely held up,
already hints at the sensuality that
would permeate sculpture in the
centuries to come.

◀ **27** *Victory of Samothrace*
Rhodes, circa 190 B.C., Parian marble (statue) and grey Lartos marble (base), H. 328 cm (245 cm for the Victory alone).

The mastery of movement here is spectacular: Victory incarnate struggles against the violent winds of the island of Samothrace, in the Aegean Sea, the statue's place of origin. The wet drape clinging to her torso and her gracefully unfurling wings give the statue an extraordinary dynamic feel and great sensuality.
This masterpiece of Greek sculpture, a monument built to commemorate a naval victory, stood on the prow of a galley, at the top of a rocky promontory, so everyone could witness the spectacle of its great power.

▲ *28 Sleeping hermaphrodite*

Rome, 2nd century B.C., marble, W. 169 cm; D. 89 cm.

Added to the Borghese collection in 1608, this sculpture was sold to Napoleon in 1807 along with 343 other antique pieces from the collection.

This Roman copy of an Alexandrian work from the 2nd century B.C. displays the sensuality and movement that now characterise Greek statuary. The treatment of this Hermaphrodite, an intersex being and son of Hermes and Aphrodite united forever with the body of a nymph, plays on the effect of surprise. Looking at the languid feminine body from behind, the onlooker would never suspect the presence of male genitalia on the other side of the statue. This taste for drama is typical of the Hellenistic style that characterised the last age of Greek art.

◄ 29 **Agasias of Ephesus** (1st century B.C.)
Fighting warrior, know as *The Borghese Gladiator*

Antium, circa 100 B.C., marble, H. 199 cm.

Added to the Borghese collection in 1611, this sculpture was sold to Napoleon in 1807 along with 343 other antique pieces from the collection.

This fighting hero, with a determined look, defends himself against an adversary with the shield on his left arm. As he prepares to strike back, his gesture leads him into a remarkable forward movement that stretches his whole body and gives him all the vigour and power of the victor. The special care taken over the minute details of his muscles is proof of the special interest shown by Greek sculpture in idealising figures. This one is meant to demonstrate strength and beauty.

▲ *30 Portrait of Alexander the Great,* called *Hermes Azara*

Tivoli, 1st-2nd century A.D., marble, H. 68 cm.

Unearthed in 1779 during excavations overseen by the Knight of Azara, the Spanish ambassador in Rome, who gave this bust to Napoleon in 1803.

The art of portraiture appeared in Greece in the 4th century B.C. and was mainly dominated by the sculptor Lysippus, a portraitist at the court of Alexander the Great, who produced many busts of the conqueror. This sculpture, a Roman copy of the head of a bronze Greek statue made by Lysippus in around 330 B.C., presents the sovereign with youthful and relatively idealised features, at the height of his glory - proof that the portrait, as an affirmation of power, was undoubtedly one of his instruments from the outset.

Rome and Etruria

In the 2nd century B.C., the Greek cities began to lose their power and decline in favour of Rome and the empire the Romans were preparing to build. The art that developed there soon moved away from the Greek depictions, which were characterised by a small number of canons and ideal figures: it focussed on creating individual characters, and placed great importance on portraiture, a legacy of Etruscan art, its direct predecessor in the region.

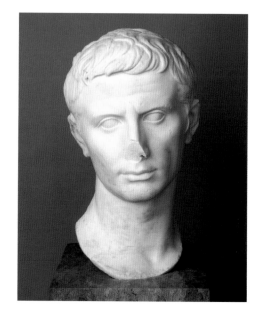

▶ **31** *Portrait of Augustus* (Emperor from 27 B.C. to 14 A.D.)
Rome, circa 5 A.D., marble, H. 36.2 cm.

In Rome, portraiture was one of the official art forms, and was the main instrument of the imperial cult that conveyed an idealised image of the sovereign throughout the Empire. The Emperor Augustus, founder of the regime, attached a number of values to his person, which his effigies were meant to exalt: the finely chiselled features, determined gaze and benevolent attitude of this bust, a real political manifesto, convey the ideas of balance, measure and authority associated with the exercise of power.

▼ **32** *Ara Pacis*
Rome, 13-9 B.C., marble, H. 114 cm, W. 147 cm (Campana collection).

This fragment of a relief comes from the Altar of Peace erected by the Senate in honour of Emperor Augustus, on the Field of Mars in Rome. A sculpted frieze ran all around the monument, similar to the one in the Parthenon, but featuring a procession of real people whose portraits are easily identifiable. It is in fact the Emperor, his family and the high dignitaries of the Empire. This imperial propaganda image, which is reminiscent of the balance and measure of classical Greek art, presents the Emperor as a guardian of peace and order in the world.

▶ **33** *Paleo-Christian mosaic: tiling from the central nave of the Church of St. Christopher*
Qabr Hiram, 6th century A.D., limestone, marble, mosaic and glass paste, 530 x 410 cm.

Roman interior decoration was very refined. Mosaic art, which consists of placing small coloured squares side by side in cement, became an essential feature of architectural decoration. This tiling adorned the floor of the central nave in a Lebanese church. It presents hunting scenes and other farming activities, in medallions formed by vine leaves, as a way of reminding the faithful of their daily work and also of honouring God through His creations.

▼ **34** *Campana plaque:*
two spirits carrying a woman
Cerveteri, 530-520 B.C., coloured terracotta, 113 x 58 cm.

The forms and conventions of Roman art originated with the productions of Etruscan civilisation, its predecessor in the region, as shown by this painted terracotta plaque that once adorned the walls of a tomb. In this picture of two spirits and a woman, heavily influenced by the Greek canons, we see the desire for individualised figures that would profoundly influence Roman art, which was less concerned with idealising the body than with portraiture.

▶ **35** *Spouses' coffin*
Cerveteri, late 6th century B.C., terracotta, H. 114 cm, W. 190 cm (Campana collection).

Found in the middle of the 19th century, broken in several pieces, in a tomb at an Etruscan necropolis in Cerveteri, this item was acquired by Napoleon III in 1861.

Etruscan statuary mainly used terracotta, especially in the area of funerary art, where it was used for large coffins in the shape of semi-recumbent figures, like this one. The depiction of this couple, who were probably from an aristocratic background, once more shows the taste for individualised characters that influenced Roman depictions.

▶ **36** *Boscoreale treasure*
Boscoreale, late 1st century B.C. - 79 A.D., silver.

Discovered in the cistern of a Roman villa near Pompeii, this treasure acquired by the Baron de Rothschild was given to the Louvre in 1895.

The Roman lifestyle was famously refined, as shown by this remarkable set of silver objects discovered in the cistern of a villa in Boscoreale, near Pompeii, where they had been placed to protect them from the eruption of Vesuvius. This treasure consists of utensils that were used for table service as well as grooming. Their main function was to emphasise their owners' wealth. Some pieces were designed solely for display, and sometimes included real sculptures such as busts of Roman emperors.

Middle Ages

In 476, the Roman Empire collapsed in the West: Antiquity came to an end. A period of ten centuries began, known as the "Middle Ages", during which all-powerful Christianity established its power in Europe, where kingdoms were taking shape. The sovereigns and the church saw art as a means of passing on their message and appearing to as many people as possible. Alongside this, a new civilisation was born in 622, Islam, whose influence would soon spread from the Near East to Spain: it was accompanied by original artistic practices, sometimes influenced by western creations.

Giotto di Bondone
(circa 1265-1337)
St. Francis of Assisi receiving the stigmata
[detail: St. Francis talking to the birds]
Italy, circa 1295-1300,
oil on wood, 313 x 163 cm.

Serving the sovereign

"Middle Ages" refers to the period from the 5th to the 15th century A.D., from the end of Antiquity to the start of the Renaissance. Medieval art underwent many changes and shifts, but always seemed to serve two main powers, the sovereign and the Church. Depictions of the monarch, one of the main commissioners of creative works, moved gradually away from the traditional Roman imperial busts to give rise to the first ceremonial portraits.

▼ 37 *Charlemagne* or *Charles le Chauve*
France, 9th century, bronze, H. of horseman: 19.5 cm,
H. of horse: 21 cm. From the treasury at Metz Cathedral.

Charlemagne was crowned Emperor of the West on 25 December 800, in Rome, by the Pope in person, thus establishing himself as the heir to the Roman, universal and Christian Empire. Carolingian art was inspired by the models and forms of Antiquity, which artists were able to observe in Italy. This equestrian statue, which may represent his grandson Charles le Chauve, copies the look and pose of the statue of the Roman Emperor Marcus Aurelius. Art was used by the sovereign to exalt his power and proclaim the origins he wanted to attribute to himself.

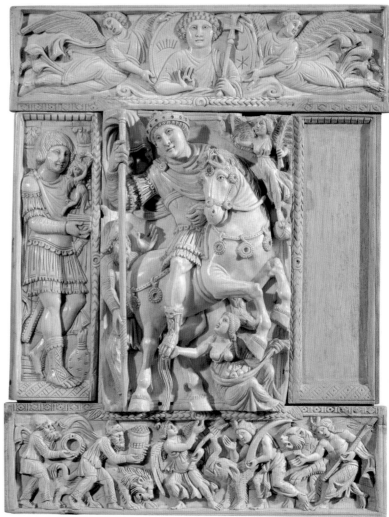

▲ 38 *The Emperor triumphant,* called *Barberini ivory*
Constantinople, 1st half of the 6th century, ivory, 34.2 x 26.8 x 2.8 cm.
Given in 1625 to the Cardinal Francesco Barberini, this leaf entered the Louvre in 1899.

The Byzantine Empire, around Constantinople, was the only part of the Roman Empire to survive the fall of Rome in 476. Like Charlemagne later, the Byzantine emperors tried to explain their attachment to the Roman model through art. This carved ivory shows a Byzantine emperor on horseback, trampling vanquished people, in a scene comparable to the old imperial Roman parades. Placed under the protection of Christ, the sovereign was supported by the Church as he established an empire as powerful as that of the Romans.

▲ 39 *Jean II le Bon, King of France*
France, circa 1350, oil on wood, 60 x 45 cm.

Recorded in the collection of Roger de Gaignères in the
17th century, this portrait was withdrawn from the sale
of the latter's estate by order of Philippe d'Orleans, who
placed it in the Royal Library.

This portrait of Jean le Bon, who reigned
from 1350 to 1364, during the Hundred
Years' War, is one of the oldest known
portraits in French painting. From the
14th century onwards, the image of the
sovereign was one of the main subjects
of pictorial representation, although for
a long time it followed the model of
antique coins and medals, which had
Roman emperors' profiles engraved
on them.

◄ 40 and 41 *Charles V, King of
France, and Queen Jeanne de Bourbon*
Île-de-France, 3rd quarter of the 14th century,
stone, 195 x 71 x 40 cm.

After the destruction of the medieval Louvre in
1658-1660, these statues were kept in the Antiques
Room of the royal Louvre.

Charles V, the son of Jean le Bon,
ascended to the throne following his
father's death, in 1364, and profoundly
revolutionised the royal image. Under
his reign, the depiction of the King
became a real instrument of power,
serving a policy designed to celebrate the
greatness of the dynasty. The aim was to
make the image visible to as many people
as possible, in particular by displaying
it on the main monuments, as is the
case for this sculpted effigy of the
royal couple, which decorated one
of the entrances to the Louvre
Castle, converted by Charles V into
an official residence.

◀ **42** *Sceptre of Charles V*
France, 1364 (?)-1380, gold, gilded silver, ruby, coloured glass, pearls, H. 53 cm.

Entrusted to the Abbey of Saint-Denis in 1380 by Charles V, this was used by all the Kings of France up to Charles X, except Charles VII and Henri IV. It entered the Louvre in 1793.

Very early on, Charles V used the arts to exalt the royal image and establish his legitimacy. He therefore had this sceptre made, a long baton topped with an emblem, an eminent symbol of power, ahead of the coronation of his son, Charles VI. On the top, placed on a fleur de lys made of gold leaf, the emblem of the French monarchy, is a representation of Charlemagne crowned, sitting on a throne. The reigning sovereign intended to link his dynasty to the memory of the Emperor of the West, after whom he was named and whose glory he wanted to remind people of.

▲ **43** Jean Fouquet
(circa 1415/1420 - between 1478/1481)
Charles VII, King of France
France, circa 1445 or 1450, oil on wood, 85 x 70 cm.

Charles VII gave his own portrait to the Sainte-Chapelle in Bourges. Louis XV added the work to the royal collections.

During the reign of Charles VII, crowned King of France in 1429 through the actions of Jeanne d'Arc, France regained the upper hand over England and put an end to the Hundred Years' War. Jean Fouquet, the most famous French painter in the late Middle Ages, painted the official portrait of the "most victorious" sovereign and gave the royal image a new lease of life: he is in fact represented with the shoulders facing forward and the head in three-quarter profile. This new posture in the history of painting gives the bust a monumental quality that contributed to the power of the King.

▲ **44** *Tomb of Philippe Pot (1428-1493), Great Seneschal of Burgundy*
Burgundy, between 1477 and 1483, limestone, 181 x 260 x 167 cm.

The funerary art of the Middle Ages also exalted the greatness and glory of the powerful ruler, who generally commissioned their tomb while they were still alive. The one made for Philippe Pot, the great lord who served the Dukes of Burgundy then the King of France, presents him in the form of a recumbent figure wearing knight's armour, carried by eight hooded mourners. These carry the coats of arms of the deceased man's noble family. This dramatised scene exalts the greatness of his family as well as his own power.

◀ **45 and 46** *Coronation sword and scabbard of the Kings of France,*
called *"Joyeuse"* or *"Charlemagne's Sword"*
France, 10th-13th century, gold, steel, glass, silver, stones, velvet, H. 105 cm, W. 22 cm.

This sword was kept in the treasury of the Abbey of Saint-Denis. It escaped the purge of royal symbols unleashed by the Revolution and entered the Louvre in 1793.

The sword symbolised nobility as the insignia of knighthood. During the coronation ceremony, the King of France was dubbed by the Archbishop of Reims, who gave him the sword called "Joyeuse", thus conferring the order of the knighthood upon him.
In the 13th century, this sword was thought to have belonged to Charlemagne, although its component parts are much more recent.
It was called "Joyeuse" in reference to The *Song of Roland*, a medieval story where it was mentioned for the first time.

Serving the divine

Along with royal imagery, the whole religious iconography of Christianity influenced the artistic creation of the Middle Ages in the West. While the image was attached to the text at first, with miniatures adorning illuminated books, it gradually became independent of it. Religious paintings illustrated various episodes of the Bible, through highly codified representations that would shape the whole history of art.

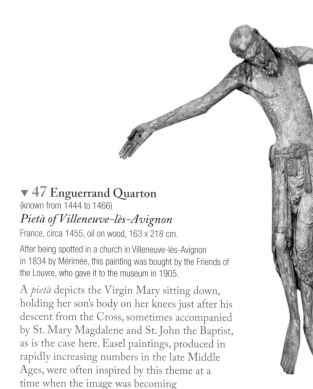

▼ 47 Enguerrand Quarton
(known from 1444 to 1466)
Pietà of Villeneuve-lès-Avignon
France, circa 1455, oil on wood, 163 x 218 cm.

After being spotted in a church in Villeneuve-lès-Avignon in 1834 by Mérimée, this painting was bought by the Friends of the Louvre, who gave it to the museum in 1905.

A *pietà* depicts the Virgin Mary sitting down, holding her son's body on her knees just after his descent from the Cross, sometimes accompanied by St. Mary Magdalene and St. John the Baptist, as is the case here. Easel paintings, produced in rapidly increasing numbers in the late Middle Ages, were often inspired by this theme at a time when the image was becoming independent of illumination, of which this work is still reminiscent with its gold background.

◄ 48 *Christ's Descent from the Cross*
Burgundy, 2nd quarter of the 12th century, polychrome gilded maple wood, 155 x 168 x 30 cm.

Given to the Louvre in 1895 by Louis Courajod, curator at the Sculptures department.

This Christ is depicted in a pose comparable to the *Pietà of Villeneuve-lès-Avignon*, although this predates it, showing the permanence of the conventions that governed religious depictions in the Middle Ages. Christ is still on the Cross, but he is already dead and his right arm is falling down slightly; this sculpture shows his faithful followers taking him down in order to bury him, watched by the Virgin, St. John, St Mary Magdalene and many other onlookers.

▼ 49 *Porphyry vase*, called *Eagle of Suger*
Vase: Egypt or imperial Rome, mount: Saint-Denis, before 1147, red porphyry, silver, 43.1 x 27 cm.

Abbot Suger, advisor to the Kings Louis VI and Louis VII, undertook to rebuild the Abbey Church of Saint-Denis, which he made into one of the first examples of the Gothic style that would become popular throughout the 13th century. He believed that religious art should be rich, opulent and lavishly decorated, for only by contemplating splendid objects could the faithful become closer to God. He had a series of liturgical vases made for the abbey church's treasury, which included this remarkable antique porphyry vase, transformed by Suger's workshops into a golden eagle.

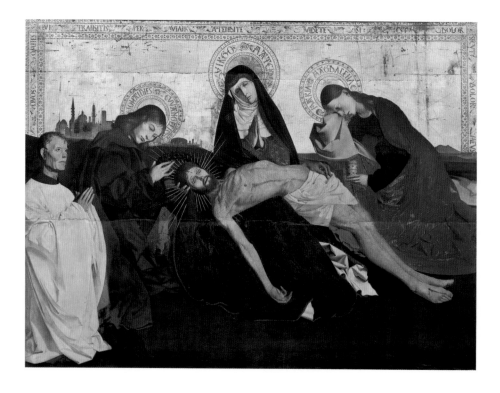

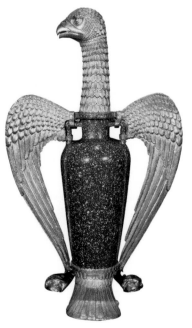

◄ **50** **Giotto di Bondone**
(circa 1265-1337)

St. Francis of Assisi receiving the stigmata
Italy, circa 1295-1300, oil on wood, 313 x 163 cm.

In the 16th century, the Florentine art historian Vasari described this altarpiece in the Church of San Francesco in Pisa. It entered the Louvre in 1813.

In the 14th century, while Gothic art was establishing itself all over Europe, Italy was the setting for totally new research that heralded the Renaissance. The Florentine painter Giotto revolutionised western painting through his studies on spatial depth, the rendering of volumes, and the character of the figures depicted. This scene, where St. Francis receives the same wounds as Christ during his crucifixion, is an example of these innovations: the image has a three-dimensional construction and seeks to represent the world with a certain sense of realism.

79

▼ **51** Cenni di Pepe, called Cimabue
(circa 1240-circa 1302)
The Virgin and Child in Majesty Surrounded by Six Angels (maestà)
Italy, circa 1280, oil on wood, 427 x 280 cm.

A *maestà* presents the Virgin Mary sitting on a throne of wisdom and holding the Baby Jesus on her knees, sometimes surrounded by angels and apostles. It is one of the major themes of the Florentine school in the 13th century, dominated by Cimabue, Giotto's teacher. With this Virgin in Majesty, we can already see the desire to break away from the absolute frontality and hieratism specific to the Byzantine icons, to give a more realistic look to the composition. The drawing is more alive, the volumes are softer and the colours are lighter.

▼ **52** *Virgin and Child from the Sainte-Chapelle*
France, circa 1260-1270, ivory, H. 41 cm.

This *Virgin* belonged to the treasury of the Sainte-Chapelle built in Paris by St. Louis, who is said to have donated it himself. Alexandre Lenoir found it during the Revolution and exhibited it for a while in his Museum of French Monuments. It was then part of the Debruge-Duménil collection and then the Soltykoff collection, before being acquired by the Louvre in 1861.

This masterpiece of Gothic art is typical of the "elegant style" that developed in Paris in the second half of the 13th century, during the reign of St. Louis. Where Italian artists were still influenced by the rigour of the Byzantine icons, French art preferred figures with swaying hips, fine facial features and gentle smiles, which are seen in many devotional statues produced by the Parisian workshops. This *Virgin and Child* thus embodies the feminine ideal of Gothic sculpture, which made it a real model, often imitated but never equalled.

◄ 53 Guido di Pietro, called Fra Angelico (known from 1417-1455)
Coronation of the Virgin
Italy, circa 1430-1432, oil on wood, 209 x 206 cm.

This altarpiece is among the works selected in 1811 for the Napoleon Museum, which displayed all the finest works from conquered Europe.

The influence of the graceful, delicate silhouettes of the Gothic era can still be seen in this panel by Fra Angelico, which depicts one of the recurring themes of medieval art: the moment when the Virgin Mary, after her Assumption, is crowned Queen of Heaven by her son Jesus Christ. Nonetheless, the desire to place the composition in a three-dimensional space, and the realism of the figures, testify to a complete mastery of the recent techniques developed in Florence, and herald the innovations of the Italian Renaissance.

54 Jan Van Eyck (circa 1390/1395-1441)
The Virgin of Chancellor Rolin
Circa 1435, oil on wood, 66 x 62 cm.
See the following double page.

▼ 55 Rogier Van der Weyden (circa 1399-1464)
Triptych of the Braque Family, circa 1435-1440, oil on wood, 41 x 136 cm.
Painted in Brussels for a Polish banker who sent it to Italy, this triptych can be found in the collection of the Dukes of Savoy. It was seized in Turin in 1799 by French troops.

Rogier Van der Weyden is the other great Flemish Primitive who, like Van Eyck, replaced the traditional golden background with a panoramic landscape, which was a great innovation in the depiction of religious figures. Christ, the Virgin Mary and St. John the Evangelist occupy the central panel, St. John the Baptist, the left panel, and St. Mary Magdalene the right panel. They are all portrayed with great realism and their fine features and drapes would profoundly influence the Italian artists.

54 Jan Van Eyck (circa 1390/1395 - 1441)
The Virgin of Chancellor Rolin Circa 1435, oil on wood, 66 x 62 cm.

Commissioned circa 1432-1435 for a chapel in Autun, where it stayed until 1793, this painting was taken during the Revolution, and sent to the Louvre in 1800.

In the 1420s, Flemish painters like Jan Van Eyck began a revolution in forms and techniques, which set them apart from the other European artists: the introduction of landscape, use of oil paints, perspective and transparent layers of paint were a few of their contributions.

This votive panel was commissioned by the very powerful Chancellor of the Duke of Burgundy, Nicolas Rolin (1376-1462), for his chapel at Autun Church. He had himself depicted, on the left, praying opposite the Virgin and Child, in a sacred space reminiscent of the loggias of Italian buildings. Behind them, a vast landscape stretches out, one of the first in the history of painting, reflecting the conception of the world in the 15th century: on the left, next to the Chancellor, we see a simple town, with its fields, evoking the earthly world of agriculture, people and everyday life. On the right, however, we see the world of the heavens, represented by a city with many bell towers. A river winds its way between them, with a simple bridge across it, the symbol of the passage the Chancellor has to make to reach piety.

Sumptuous fabrics

The fabrics and brocades worn by the Chancellor Rolin have been depicted with extreme refinement and precision, made possible by the use of oil paints which Van Eyck perfected. In the 15th century, Flemish Realism was famous for the dense, delicate contours obtained by the painter here.

A divine blessing

The aged face of the Baby Jesus foreshadows his tragic fate, his death on the Cross at the age of 33. Here, he carries the globus cruciger (cross-bearing orb) symbolising the reign of Christianity over the world, and blesses the praying Chancellor with a simple gesture. At the same time he seems to touch the bridge in the background with his finger, as if inviting Rolin to join him.

Up on the wall

These two figures contemplating the landscape from the top of a wall are surprising because of the central place they occupy in the composition. Seen from behind, they enable the spectator to project themselves into the depth of the picture, in order to join them in looking through the window on the world which painting offers.

The mysterious island

In the distance, this mysterious island in the middle of the river seems inaccessible. A boat full of rowers is only just managing to reach it. Is it the image of heavenly Jerusalem, an ideal city that awaits all believers deserving of divine salvation?

Islam in the medieval world

A hundred years after its advent in 622, Islam conquered the territories between India and Spain. Until the 15th century, the Iberian Peninsula was totally and then partially Muslim; new art forms developed there, blending western and North African influences. At the same time, Iran and the Near East were two important creative centres, working with new techniques that Europeans had not yet fully mastered.

▶ 56 *Pyxis of al-Mughira*
Spain, 968, elephant ivory, sculpted, engraved decoration, H. 16 cm, diam. 11.8 cm.

During the reign of Abd al-Rahman III (929-961), the caliphate of Cordoba, in Spain, was a centre for intense intellectual and artistic activity, marked by abundant production of sculpted ivory, as shown by this small box called a "pyxis". This was given to the Caliph's son, Prince al-Mughira, and its highly symbolic decoration evokes the power of the reigning Umayyad dynasty. The sovereign, sitting on the left, is being entertained by a lute player and carries the traditional emblems: a bottle and a braided sceptre made from plants.

◀ 57 *Lion from Monzón with an articulated tail*
Spain, 12th-13th century, cast bronze, engraved decoration,
H. 31.5 cm, length 54.5 cm.

In the 12th and 13th centuries, the great caliphate of Cordoba no longer existed: in the south of the Iberian Peninsula, it was followed by a multitude of small kingdoms called taifas. Muslim Hispania was no longer famous for its ivory work, but rather for its bronze art, as exemplified by this remarkable lion sculpture, entirely covered with a fine engraving of plant patterns. It seems to have been used as a fountain, as indicated by its gaping mouth, ready to spit out water.

▲ 58 *Epigraph dish*
Iran, late 12th - early 13th century,
ceramic (silica paste), painted and metallic
lustre decoration on opaque glaze,
gold highlights (petit feu, haft-rang, minai),
diam. (min) 8.1 cm, diam. (opening) 22 cm,
thickness (of base) 0.4 cm.

At the same time, in Iran, potters
were developing particularly
advanced ceramic procedures,
well before the Europeans,
enabling them to make drawings
of great precision like this one.
The pattern, a prince on
horseback with a falcon on his
fist, is a recurring subject in the
Muslim iconographic repertoire,
and is partly inspired by Persian
and Arabic poetry. In terms of
precision, the delicate shades and
lustre decoration with gold
highlights seen in this depiction
have nothing to envy the
illuminated miniatures borrowed
from book art.

▶ 59 *Cladding panel*
Iran, second half of the 13th century,
ceramic, decoration on glaze,
metallic lustre, 78.5 x 49.5 cm.

Throughout the 13th century,
ceramic was undoubtedly among
the most commonly practised art
forms in the Middle East,
especially in Iran, where it was
used to create opulent interior
decorations.
The use of ceramic as a wall
cladding was seen as an eminent
symbol of wealth at the time, and
conferred great prestige on the
commissioner. This set of tiles
comes from a mausoleum whose
walls were covered with these
depictions of animals, plants and
sometimes people, surrounded by
poetic or religious verses.
Together, they evoke the cycle of
nature, whose permanence is
opposed to death and helps
lessen its sorrow.

▲ 60 *Basin* called
"Baptistère de Saint Louis"

Syria or Egypt, circa 1330-1340,
copper alloy engraved decoration inlaid
with silver, gold and black paste,
H. 23.5 cm, max. diam. 50.5 cm.

This basin was part of the treasure of the
Sainte-Chapelle at Vincennes Castle.

This large basin was made half a
century after the death of St. Louis.
For a long time it was part of the
French royal collections, and it
was used in 1601 for the baptism
of the future Louis XIII. The
procession of figures surrounding
it and the abundant details that
adorn its sides depict hunting
and fighting scenes: it features a
falconer, princes on horseback
and even a man holding a cheetah
on a lead. These recurring patterns
in Muslim art are given an
exceptional treatment here, which
shows great mastery of metal art.

▶ 61 *Celestial globe*

Iran, 1144, cast brass, engraved decoration
inlaid with silver, globe diam. 17.5 cm.

In the Muslim world, scholars
were very active and amassed an
incomparable body of knowledge
throughout the Middle Ages,
based on the science of the
Ancients. In the area of
astronomy, the system devised by
the Greek Ptolemy, whose works
written in the 2nd century A.D.
were translated into Arabic in
the 7th century, dominated
depictions of the sky. In order to
make this celestial globe, which
displays 48 constellations and
states the exact position of 1 025
stars, the astronomer Yunus ibn
al-Husayn al-Asturlabi worked
with the Greek scholar's
calculations, adapting and
sometimes correcting them.

Renaissance

In the late 15th century in Florence, a real revolution took place in the arts, letters and western thought as a whole. Governed by the Medicis, the Tuscan city was home to "humanist" philosophers who returned to the Antique ideal of order and beauty. Artists like Botticelli, Uccello and Donatello, then Da Vinci, Michelangelo and Raphael were inspired by this reflection and revived a depiction of the world which benefited from contributions by Cimabue, Giotto and Fra Angelico. During the wars in Italy, this cultural movement reached France and the Northern countries, which experienced their own "Renaissance"...

Leonardo Da Vinci (1452-1519)
*The Virgin and Child with
St. Anne* [detail]
Italy, circa 1501-1513, oil on poplar wood,
168 x 130 cm.

The Renaissance in Italy

In the 15th century, Italy was the birthplace of a vast cultural movement that gradually moved away from medieval art, the "Renaissance". It sought to revive the Antique culture in all its aspects, and return to the ideal of order and beauty attached to the Greco-Roman model. The Renaissance was also characterised by the search for ways to imitate the truth of the world. New procedures were developed for this purpose, such as perspective.

▼ **62 Andrea Mantegna** (1431-1506)
The Crucifixion

Italy, 1456-1459, oil in wood, 76 x 96 cm.

Brought from Verona by the French army, this triptych entered the Louvre in 1798. The main panels were returned in 1815 and the predella was dismantled. The *Crucifixion*, at the centre, remains at the Louvre.

This crucifixion follows a rigorous composition that divides the space in two parts, separated at the centre by the figure of Jesus Christ: to his right, the good thief and the saints represent goodness; to his left, the bad thief and Roman soldiers embody evil. Behind the figures, this construction aims to create a sense of depth by giving a spherical aspect to the hill of Golgotha, where Jesus was martyred. The landscape shows real archaeological attention which, like the careful treatment of the drapes, marks the return to the ideal of order attached to the Antique model.

◄ **63 Donatello** (1386-1466)
The Virgin and Child

Italy, 15th century, polychrome gilded terracotta, 102 x 74 cm.

This high relief is said to come from the Chapel of San Lorenzo in Vigliano (Tuscany).It was acquired in 1881 from a Florentine antiquarian.

The influence of Gothic statuary can still be seen in the pathetic expression on the face of this Virgin Mary, who holds Baby Jesus in her arms and displays a palpable sense of anguish. Donatello nonetheless applied the rules of the new science of perspective to the art of sculpture, and added thickness to his composition in order to construct three successive planes in depth: the seat, the people and then the golden drape that forms the backdrop. It gives the figures a density which is absent from medieval images and helps convey their emotions.

▲ **64 Paolo Uccello** (1397-1475)
The Battle of San Romano, Italy, oil on wood, 182 x 317 cm.

This picture is part of a set of three panels, probably commissioned by Lionardo Bartolini Salimbeni circa 1435 in Uccello. Between 1479 and 1486, Lorenzo de Medici ordered the three *Battles* to be placed in his new palace in Florence. The panel in the Louvre was acquired in 1863 with the Campana collection.

This panel depicts the Florentines' victory over the Sienese in June 1432. The image gains a sense of movement, which was unknown in medieval depictions and divides the soldiers' departure for the battle field into three progressive stages: from left to right, the knights gallop off, the lances are lowered, and the troops move off. Above all, it aims to create the illusion of depth; Uccello was in fact one of the first to carry out in-depth research into perspective. He thus shows the knight on the right "foreshortened" in order to fit him into a three-dimensional space.

▶ **65 Sandro Botticelli**
(1445-1510)

Venus and the Graces offering Gifts to a Young Girl

Italy, circa 1483, fresco, 211 x 283 cm.

This fresco, discovered in 1873 in a villa near Florence, was sold by a Florentine antiquarian. The Louvre bought it in 1882.

Renaissance artists sought to return to the ideal of beauty specific to the figures of Antiquity: this fresco thus shows Venus, on the left, accompanied by the Three Graces, who together embody the archetype of feminine perfection. Their long hair and pronounced hips are in contrast with the more rigid forms of the young girl, on the right, who is receiving a gift from the deities. Influenced by a philosophy that draws on the great texts of Plato, Botticelli perhaps depicted this gift as an allegory of the "ideal beauty" that mortals could now experience.

▲ **66 Pisanello** (before 1395-1455)
*Male bearded reedling, depicted once in flight and twice on the
ground*, Italy, 15th century, watercolour, brown ink, fountain pen (drawing), white
highlights, vellum (paper), 11.7 x 15.5 cm.

The Renaissance saw a return to the imitation of nature. Greek
painters tried to create the illusion of reality: Italian artists gradually
succeeded in this, using innovative and sometimes very skillful
techniques. Pisanello carried out considerable research into
composition and made nature studies to achieve this ideal.

▶ **67 Leonardo da Vinci** (1452-1519)
The Virgin and Child with St. Anne
Italy, circa 1501-1513, oil on poplar wood, 168 x 130 cm.

Leonardo da Vinci kept this work until his death in 1519. François I probably acquired it but it
only appeared in the royal inventories in the 17th century.

Da Vinci learned from the experiments of previous years, as shown by
the perspective at the back of the picture. Heralding the maturity of the
Italian Renaissance in the 16th century, he also developed the psychology
of his characters to give them more density. Sitting on her mother
St. Anne's lap, the Virgin restrains Jesus with a maternal gesture, as he is
about to mount the lamb who symbolises his future crucifixion.

▼ **68 Jacopo Bellini** (1400-1470/1471)
Funeral of the Virgin, Italy, 15th century, brown ink, fountain pen (drawing), vellum (paper), 38 x 26 cm.
The Italian Renaissance perfected the construction of three-dimensional spaces thanks to the
contribution of mathematical science: perspective was now organised around a vanishing point
located on a horizon line, towards which all the lines in the picture converged. In this scene of the
Virgin's entombment by the apostles, the Venetian painter and draughtsman Jacopo Bellini used
the alignment of the characters in the procession to emphasise depth and show the origin of the
procession: the door opening onto a fantastical city, at the back of the drawing.

▶ **69 Leonardo da Vinci**
(1452-1519)
The Monna Lisa
Italy, circa 1503-1506, oil on poplar wood,
77 x 53 cm.

In 1516, Leonardo da Vinci arrived in France
with this painting, invited by François I.
The King acquired it after his death from his
heir, Salai. On 21 August 1911, it was stolen
by an Italian craftsman and was found two
years later.

Leonardo da Vinci was one of the
first artists to break away from the
hieratism of medieval portraits like
that of Jean II le Bon (see notice
39), where the subject is painted in
profile on a golden background: the
wife of Francesco del Giocondo is
shown here from the waist up, in
three-quarter profile, sitting in a
loggia that opens onto a fantastical
landscape. The enigmatic smile of
this universal icon, which helped
make the work famous, expresses
the inner serenity of the woman
known as "Monna Lisa". This
fleeting expression captured by the
artist is also the symbol of art's
struggle against the ephemerality
of the world around it.

▲ **70 Raffaello Santi, called Raphael** (1483-1520)
Portrait of Baldassare Castiglione, writer and diplomat (1478-1529)
Italy, 1514-1515, oil on canvas, 82 x 67 cm.

Probably painted in Rome on the occasion of Castiglione's appointment as ambassador to the Pope Leon X by the Duke of Urbino, this picture comes from the Louis XIV collections.

Heavily influenced by Da Vinci, whom he met in Florence, Raphael presents the poet and courtier Balthazar Castiglione in a pose similar to the Monna Lisa. The sobriety of the costume, absence of decoration and soft light give this portrait an air of great simplicity, which was fundamental to the artist's pictorial principles. The same principles govern the rigour of a composition that draws the spectator's attention to the character's face and gaze.

◄ **71 Michelangelo Buonarroti, called Michelangelo** (1475-1564)
The Dying Slave [one of two *Slaves*, with *The Rebellious Slave*]
Italy, 1513-1515, marble, 209 x 228 cm.

Michelangelo gave the two *Slaves* to Roberto Strozzi, in exile in Florence at the time, who in turn gave them to François I. It was probably Henri II, the Dauphin, who then gave them to the Constable of Montmorency for his castle in Écouen. The *Slaves* then went to Richelieu's castle before being seized during the Revolution and entering the Louvre in 1794.

Apart from innovations in painting, the Italian Renaissance was very interested in anatomical research aimed at reviving the ideal of beauty found in Antique sculptures. Here, the twisting body evokes the sensuality and movement of Greek statues. However, the meaning of these slaves, made for the tomb of Pope Jules II, is uncertain: an allegory of the provinces conquered by the sovereign pontiff, or a symbol of enslaved human passions?

▶ **72 Leonardo da Vinci** (1452-1519)
The Virgin of the Rocks
Italy, circa 1483-1486, oil on wood transposed onto canvas, 199 x 122 cm.

This picture was intended for the Church of San Francesco Grande, but another version, the one preserved today at the National Gallery in London, was put there. This one was most probably bought by Louis XII.

This composition encloses the characters in a harmonious pyramid: the Virgin pushes St. John the Baptist, whom she holds by the shoulder, towards Baby Jesus, while an angel points at him. A chiaroscuro erases the contrasts between light and shade: the contours and space emerge from the half-darkness, which reinforces the mysterious atmosphere of this panel. It is in fact the light that sculpts the characters, in an approach to painting that would appeal to other contemporary artists, such as Raphael.

◀ **73 Raffaello Santi, called Raphael** (1483-1520) *The Virgin and Child with the Young St. John the Baptist* called *The Beautiful Gardener*

Italy, 1507 or 1508, oil on poplar wood, 122 x 80 cm.

Comes from the collections of François I.

Raphael borrowed the theme and pyramidal composition of The *Virgin of the Rocks* by Da Vinci, transporting it to a country landscape in the middle of a meadow. Baby Jesus tries to catch the book containing his future, and looks at his mother with curiosity. The little St. John the Baptist watches him but the Virgin restrains him, as if to protect him from a painful revelation. These gestures and looks make the atmosphere much more serene than in the disturbing compositions of Leonardo and develop the sense of harmony typical of the Renaissance in its mature phase.

▶ 74 Vittore Carpaccio
(1472-1525/1526)
*The Sermon of St. Stephen
at Jerusalem*
Italy, 1514 (?), oil on canvas,
148 x 194 cm.

The 15th century was a golden
age for Venetian painting,
which followed its own path
within the Italian Renaissance.
Colour took on considerable
importance in drawing and the
chromatic scale used structured
the works into planes and
spaces. In this panel by
Carpaccio, the treatment of the
fabrics worn by St. Stephen and
the varied audience to whom he
is preaching make the
characters stand out from the
architectural background,
depicted in pearly white and
sometimes ochre tones. Colour
therefore creates a sense of
depth here.

▶ 75 Attributed to
Tiziano Vecellio,
called Titian (1488/1490-1576)
Pastoral Concert
Italy, circa 1509, oil on canvas,
105 x 136 cm.

From the collections of Louis XIV,
this work was transferred to the Louvre
in 1792.

This landscape evokes the
mythical paradise of the
Greeks, Arcadia, which greatly
inspired the artists of the
Renaissance. This natural,
serene and harmonious setting
features two musicians, totally
oblivious to the nude nymphs
on either side of them. Should
this scene be understood as the
allegory of Poetry which the
two young people are inspired
to create by the muses, the
product of their imagination?

76 Paolo Caliari, called Veronese (1528-1588)
The Wedding at Cana Italy, 1562-1563, oil on canvas, 666 x 990 cm.

This canvas was painted for the refectory in the Benedictine convent of San Giorgio Maggiore in Venice, built by Palladio. It was transported to the Louvre by French troops in 1798.
After the fall of the Empire in 1815, instead of being returned to Venice, it was exchanged for a canvas by Le Brun, *The Magdalene and the Pharisee.*

Veronese painted this canvas, the biggest one preserved by the Louvre, to adorn the refectory of the San Giorgio Maggiore convent in Venice. During a wedding feast in Galilee, there was not enough wine to finish the meal. Jesus ordered the servants to fill six jars of water, then to serve the host, who was surprised to see that the water had turned into wine. This was the first miracle accomplished by Christ.
This sacred episode is transposed here into the splendid setting of a Venetian wedding in the Renaissance: the Antique-style decoration, the characters' luxurious costumes, the precious crockery, and the servants and musicians show this is an important event. Among the 130 guests, we see biblical figures, of course, but also certain political personalities of the time, as well as a few artists. In the centre, Christ and the Virgin Mary preside over the scene, the apostles at their sides. The married couple and their guests surround them. Behind the balustrade, the cooks are busy, while servants, dwarves and jesters bustle about the table. Venetian lords and ladies watch the scene from the upper gallery.

The Mother and the Son

Jesus and the Virgin Mary take the place of the married couple, in the middle of the table. With an inscrutable face, at the centre of a composition teeming with people and little events, Christ appears in absolute frontality, emphasising his divine nature.

Foreshadowing the Passion

Right at the centre of the picture, just above Christ's head, a butcher carves a piece of lamb, yet the dessert has already been served on the table. This scene foreshadows Jesus' fate and his coming Passion: he is the sacrificial lamb, the agnus Dei.

The married couple

The actual married couple occupy the far left of the composition and are relegated to the end of the table by the painter. Richly attired in 16th-century Venetian fashions, they seem absent from the events but still attract the attention of all the people around them.

Painters and musicians

In front of the main table is a group of four musicians, who appeared to the commentators of the 17th century as being portraits of Veronese and his friends, the Venetian painters Bassano, Tintoretto and Titian. On the small table, an hourglass is running out, emphasising the idea of the passing of time and the coming end.

The Renaissance in France and the Northern countries

The Renaissance arrived in France via the wars in Italy led by the Kings Charles VIII, Louis XII and François I. The latter even invited some Italian artists to his court, like Leonardo da Vinci, whose work he financially supported. In the Northern countries, however, the Renaissance seems to have followed its own path and developed almost independently; yet, it engaged in a fruitful dialogue with works of art from Italy.

◄ **77 Jean Clouet**
(circa 1480 - 1540/1541)
François I, King of France
France, circa 1530, oil on wood,
96 x 74 cm.

François I commissioned this portrait from Jean Clouet circa 1530. The painting would remain in the royal collections and enter the Louvre in 1793.

François I discovered the Italian painters during his military expeditions and invited the most talented among them to his court: he thus imported the Renaissance into French territory and provided patronage on an unprecedented level. Clouet, the King's official painter, produced this portrait containing references to the effigies of Raphael and Leonardo, as shown by the treatment of the hands and light, the facial volumes and the brilliance of opulent jewels. Here, the King has no need to display the traditional symbols attached to his function in order to express his power.

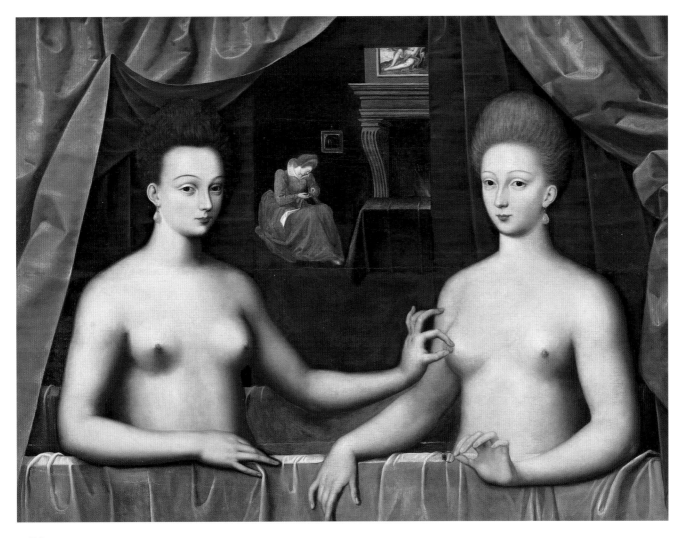

▲ 78 **Fontainebleau School**
Portrait presumed to be of Gabrielle d'Estrées and
her sister, the Duchess of Villars
France, circa 1594, oil on wood, 96 x 125 cm.

The French Renaissance soon freed itself from the Italian
influence, having learnt all its lessons, and was embodied in
what is customarily called the "Fontainebleau School". This
developed a pronounced taste for enigma, as shown by this
strange picture which depicts the Duchess of Villars
pinching the breast of her sister, Gabrielle d'Estrées, mistress
of Henry IV. This curious gesture undoubtedly refers to
Gabrielle's pregnancy, but above all accentuates the sensuality
of a scene that was already legitimised by the bathing theme.

▶ 79 **Hans Memling** (circa 1435 - 1494)
The Virgin and Child with St. James and St. Dominic
Northern Schools, circa 1488-1490, oil on wood, 130 x 160 cm.

In the 15th century, Flemish painting underwent its own
Renaissance and developed its own principles, established by
the works of Van Eyck and Van der Weyden (see notices 54
and 55). The followers of these two great artists, who included
Memling, maintained this specific kind of painting,
characterised by the detailed treatment of the landscapes, the
refinement of the drapes and the realism of the compositions.
This scene showing a group praying to the Virgin Mary
brilliantly illustrates the mastery of these innovations.

◄ **80 Quentin Metsys**
(circa 1465/1466-1530)
The Gold Weigher and his Wife
Northern Schools, 1514, oil on wood,
71 x 68 cm.

This picture belonged to Rubens
and was then acquired by the Louvre
in 1806 at a public sale.

Italian and Flemish painting
kept influencing each other
throughout the 16th century:
Metsys brought the lessons of
Da Vinci to Flanders and gave
his characters a psychological
dimension, while carefully
depicting their hands and
gestures. This scene, where a
banker's activity distracts his
wife from her spiritual reading,
nonetheless acts as a moral
warning against avarice.

▶ **81 Gregor Erhart**
(1470-1540)
St. Mary Magdalene
Northern Schools, 1510, limewood,
original polychromy, stand and front part
of the feet restored in the 19th century,
177 x 44 x 43 cm.

The Renaissance also reached
the Northern countries in the
16th century, where the new
forms developed by the Italian
artists were assimilated and
combined with the specific
tastes of the Flemish and
German traditions. With her
nudity and harmonious
proportions, this St. Mary
Magdalene shows the legacy
of Botticelli's female figures,
characterised by their long hair
and sensually swaying hips. Her
modesty nonetheless remains
faithful to the late Gothic style,
which still persisted in these
areas of Europe.

▲ **82 Albrecht Dürer** (1471-1528)
Self-portrait or *Portrait of the Artist Holding a Thistle*
Germany, 1493, parchment glued to canvas, 56 x 44 cm.

At a very young age, Albrecht Dürer travelled to Venice, where he discovered
a radically new conception of the world and the artist's role. From then on, he
strove to become aware of his own status and began to depict himself, as an artist,
through a series of self-portraits. The thistle he holds in his hand here is probably
a reference to Christ's crown of thorns and may associate Jesus' martyrdom with
the creator's suffering, whose role has something of a divine mission about it.

▲ **83 Hans Holbein the Younger**
(1497-1543)
Erasmus
Northern Schools, circa 1523, oil on wood, 43 x 33 cm.

Initially part of the collection of Charles I, King of
England, this portrait entered the Everhard Jabach
collection before it was acquired by Louis XIV in 1671.

Erasmus was one of the humanist
intellectuals of the Renaissance who
sought to reconcile the study of Antique
texts with the teaching of the Christian
Gospels. Very early on, the painter
Holbein, heavily influenced by Dürer, was
one of his friends and painted a series of
three portraits of him (to which this one
belongs). Erasmus, busy writing his
Commentary on the Gospel according to
St. Mark, is depicted here in profile, in the
great tradition of the Roman imperial
medals: the artist thus made the man of
letters as important as the sovereign.

▶ **84 Hieronymus Bosch** (circa 1450-1516)
Ship of Fools
Northern Schools, circa 1510-1515, oil on wood,
58 x 33 cm.

Aboard a frail raft flying the flag of the
devil, two clergymen surrounded by
numerous companions indulge in vice and
lust: the pleasures of the bottle, gluttony,
stupidity and heresy are caricatured in this
allegory, whose satirical treatment does
not hide the moral condemnation.
This fantastical aspect, specific to Bosch's
work, would influence the Flemish artists
of the Mannerist movement throughout
the 16th century.

Mannerism

Vasari, the first Art historian, calls "manner" any features of an artist expression. The painters, now able to copy the world perfectly, are looking forward, during the 16th century, to express their passions and feelings, to show their character. The bodies are stretched, the figures torturous, the compositions overloaded. Mannerism calls the different innovations of the coming centuries and builds a bridge between the Renaissance and the Baroque periods.

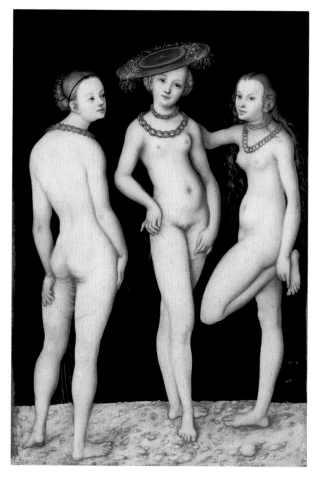

▲ **85 Giuseppe Arcimboldo**
(1527-1593)
Autumn
Italy, circa 1573, oil on canvas, 76 x 64 cm.

Commissioned in 1573 by Maximilian II of Habsburg, the *Seasons* series was discovered at an antique dealer's in Lyon in the 1950s, then bought by the Louvre in 1964.

Mannerism is first and foremost characterised by a pronounced taste for the decorative aspect of compositions. In this allegory of autumn, the Milanese painter Arcimboldo assembles all kinds of objects, flowers and fruits, a few cereals and even a vine leaf, creating a strange human face. The association of humans and nature to which the Renaissance ideal aspired is celebrated in this depiction, which evokes the time of the grape harvest and therefore drinking.

▶ **86 Lucas Cranach the Elder**
(1472-1553)
The Three Graces
Northern Schools, circa 1531, oil on wood, 36 x 24 cm.

In this work, Cranach interprets the Antique theme of the Three Graces, whom he represents in the same way as the Venuses he painted in a series of successful portraits: teenagers with stretched out bodies, whose snowy whiteness contrasts with the dark background, wear accessories that make their nudity all the more striking. The irony in this composition, which transgresses the extreme codification of Renaissance images, is specific to the Mannerist style.

▶ **87 Domenico Theotocopoulos, called El Greco**
(1541-1614)
Christ on the Cross Adored by Two Donors
Spain, circa 1590, oil on canvas, 260 x 171 cm.

Among the paintings in the Spanish Gallery put together by Louis-Philippe, this work was the only one to be returned to the Louvre in 1908, after being auctioned in London in 1853.

The cold, deliberately strident colours and excessively elongated body of Christ align this work with the Mannerist movement. However, the refusal of perspective, shown in this composition which replaces the traditional landscape with a tormented, dramatic sky, takes El Greco back to his Cretan roots, and makes this work more similar to the Byzantine icons that shaped the artist's mental world.

Islamic art, from the 16th to the 18th century

In the 16th century, three Muslim empires coexisted in the Near and Middle East: the Persian Empire, the oldest, was rivalled by the Ottoman Empire, whose Sultan proclaimed himself "caliph", commander of the faithful. Meanwhile, the Mughal warriors, driven away several times, finally managed to establish their power over India. Therefore, in these three creative centres, Islamic's art production between the 16th and 18th century was characterised by extraordinary diversity.

▶ **88** *Angel Gabriel Reveals Sura VIII of the Koran to Muhammad Siyar–i Nabi*
Turkey, circa 1595, gouache and gold on paper, 28.9 x 27.3 cm.

In 1753, this belonged to Princess Se'adetlü Bâsh-Rûkhshâh Kadin, then Major R.G. Gayer-Anderson until 1939. The Louvre acquired it at a public sale in 1984.

From the middle of the 15th century, the East Mediterranean was dominated by the vast Ottoman Empire built by the Muslim Turks. Their sovereign, called a "sultan", gave himself the title of "caliph", referring to him as the successor to the prophet Mohammed and commander of the faithful. The imperial workshops therefore produced many religious calligraphies, including this illumination, taken from a *Life of the Prophet* commissioned by Sultan Murad III (1574-1595). It depicts a key episode in the Muslim religion: the moment when the Angel Gabriel revealed God's message to Mohammed, that of the Koran.

◀ **89** *Dagger with a horse's head hilt*

India, 17th century, blade: steel, decoration inlaid with gold, handle: jade, carved decoration, inlaid with gold and semi-precious stones, 50.5 cm.

Part of the old Salomon de Rothschild collection, this dagger was acquired in 1927 by legacy by the Louvre.

Between the 16th and 18th centuries, another great Muslim empire was established in India, that of the Mughal warriors. The art that developed there shows a profound fascination with jade, thought to have protective properties: the objects carved from this costly material enjoyed incomparable prestige at the imperial court. For example, this was the case with the daggers carved with horses, like this one: the extreme refinement of the depiction, delicate precious stone inlay and gold thread highlights at the base of the blade make this parade weapon an eminent symbol of wealth and power.

▲ **90** *Carpet "from Mantes"* [detail], Iran, late 16th century, wool, asymmetric knot, 780 x 385 cm.
From Mantes collegiate church, acquired by the Louvre in 1912.

At the end of the 16th century, the imperial workshops of Muslim Persia produced sumptuous knotted carpets, richly decorated and organised around a central medallion. Impressive in its dimensions, this work combines the recurring theme of plants and animals in nature with the old Chinese phoenix and dragon pattern, showing the influences that permeated Islamic art. A newer image is that of the hunter with his musket, a weapon only recently introduced in Persia by the Europeans. It illustrates the changes that took place between these two regions and which made it possible for this rug to come to France, where it was greatly appreciated.

وَاللَّهُ عَلَى كُلِّ شَيْءٍ قَدِيرٌ جُونْ خُوتَعَالَى حَضْرَتِنْدَنْ وَحْيِ
كَلْدِي غَنِيمَتْ مَالِنِي نِجَه اِمْدِنْ كِرَكَ اللَّهُ تَعَالَى رَسُولُنَه

17th and 18th century

17th-century art in Holland was known as the Golden Age, a sign
that this era dominated all the others. The great Dutch painters
preferred to depict everyday scenes. In Italy, Caravaggio displayed
his originality with a powerful taste for drama and chiaroscuro,
heralding the Baroque movement.
In reaction, the French painters worked to serve Louis XIV and
created the Classical style, fiercely attached to straight lines, with
harmonious lighting and sober compositions. The 18th century
evolved towards a new representation of the individual: it was time
for celebratory painting, more libertine and also more intimate,
far from any religious influence.

Maurice Quentin Delatour
(1704-1788)
*Portrait of the Marquise de
Pompadour* [detail]
France, 1755, pastel on blue paper,
175 x 128 cm.

The Dutch Golden Age

In the 17th century, the Netherlands experienced a Golden Age and became the most powerful trading force in the world. Dutch painting then enjoyed increasing popularity, and was characterised by a special attachment to indoor scenes and everyday subjects. Painters sought to seize the moment and portray the diversity of this new society that surrounded them, with great realism and spontaneity.

▶ **91 Frans Hals**
(circa 1581/1585-1666)
Buffoon with a Lute
Circa 1624-1626, oil on canvas, 70 x 62 cm.

In the Gustave de Rothschild collection since 1873, this work was given to the Louvre in lieu of inheritance tax in 1984.
This smiling lute player seems to have been caught in mid-action by Frans Hals, who gives his model an amazing presence and spontaneity. The vivacity of the features and colours gives this character amazing expressiveness and illustrates the interest in depicting everyday life that appeared in 17th-century Holland. A simple street musician or actor in costume, this young man also displays a taste for disguise and humour, which is typical of the artist's works.

▲ **93 Rembrandt Harmenszoon Van Rijn, called Rembrandt** (1606-1669)
Self-Portrait at his Easel
1660, oil on canvas, 111 x 85 cm.

Rembrandt's attachment to the human face is seen again in the many self-portraits he painted throughout his life. In this one, he is 54 years old: pronounced wrinkles, a puffy face and tired eyes show the inexorable effects of time, which the artist sought to accentuate here. A mysterious light envelops the depiction; it further emphasises his facial features, worn by the challenges of life. This lighting also gives him a melancholy, tormented look, which has characterised genius since the Renaissance: a way for the painter to affirm himself in his role, palette in hand.

▶ **92 Rembrandt Harmenszoon Van Rijn, called Rembrandt** (1606-1669)
Jesus Christ Healing the Sick, called *The One Hundred Guilder Piece*
Circa 1642-1649, engraving, drypoint and chiselling, 28 x 39.9 cm.

As well as being famous for his painting, Rembrandt was also known for his engravings, which were a considerable success during the artist's lifetime: this one, undoubtedly the most popular, achieved the exceptional price of 100 guilders, which is where its traditional title comes from. Always on the lookout for greater spontaneity in depicting the characters he wanted to give life to, the artist had a real model pose to give great sincerity and truth to this preaching figure of Christ curing the sick.

◄ 94 Pierre Paul Rubens (1577-1640)
*The Landing of Marie de Medici at Marseille,
on 3 November 1600*

1622-1625, oil on canvas, 394 x 295 cm.

The set of pictures commissioned by Marie de Medici in 1625
was transported to the Louvre for restoration in 1790,
before being exhibited in its entirety from 1815 onwards.

This work is part of the monumental series of
24 pictures commissioned by Queen Marie de
Medici, widow of Henri IV, from the Dutch
painter Pierre Paul Rubens for the two galleries at
her new palace, Palais du Luxembourg, in Paris.
Here we see the young princess setting foot on
French soil for the first time, ready to meet her
future husband; this majestic arrival is glorified
by the mythological scenes that surround the
historical composition, in a whirl of shapes that
forcefully herald the arrival of the Baroque
movement in France.

▲ 96 Antoon Van Dyck (1599-1641)
Charles I, King of England (1600–1649),
called *Charles I at the Hunt*

Circa 1635, oil on canvas, 266 x 207 cm.

Bought by Charles I in 1638, we do not know how this
picture came to France. The Countess Du Barry acquired it
for her castle in Louveciennes and then sold it to Louis XVI
in 1775.

Van Dyck was Ruben's first assistant in
Antwerp, before leaving Flanders to become
the official portraitist of the Court of England.
This sumptuous portrait of Charles I
(1600-1649) is not in keeping with the
rigidity of the affected official depictions;
it shows the Prince hunting, having
dismounted his horse, in a natural yet
distinguished pose. Behind this apparent
spontaneity, proper to Dutch painting, the
sovereign surveys his kingdom's vast
landscape, showing his greatness and the
extent of his power.

▶ 95 Jan Vermeer
(1632-1670)
The Lacemaker
Circa 1669-1670, oil on canvas,
24 x 21 cm.

This frequent theme in
Dutch literature and
painting still shows the
period's taste for indoor
scenes, the intimacy of
which is reinforced by the
small size of the painting
here. Vermeer paints a scene
penetrated by light, which
focuses the spectator's gaze
on the precise movements
of the activity in which the
young girl is engaged.
He uses optical artifices to
achieve this: the objects in
the foreground seem
deformed and vague, while
the centre of the composition
remains perfectly clear.

Baroque, Tenebrism and chiaroscuro

In Italy, the painter Caravaggio started a real revolution that overturned all the pictorial preconceptions of the time: he was famous for the violent chiaroscuros and powerful dramatisation of his paintings, which heavily influenced Spanish Tenebrist painting and the budding Baroque movement. The latter, with its taste for theatrics, the serpentine line and suspended bodies, would spread all over Europe.

▲ **98 Georges de La Tour** (1593-1652)
The Cheat, France, 1635, oil on canvas, 106 x 146 cm.
Found by the tennis player Paul Landry at a Parisian antique shop in 1926, this painting was given to the Louvre by its owner in 1972 after identification. The realistic fabrics and expressions, chiaroscuro effects and depiction of a scene from a heavily theatricalised daily life show the influence of Caravaggio's work on the painting of De La Tour and his contemporaries. A drama is playing out here: the elegant young man on the right cannot resist the three temptations that were condemned by the morals of the century: wine, the flesh and gambling. He is thus vulnerable to the cheat and the two female accomplices who are preparing to rob him.

▶ **97** Michelangelo
Merisi, called Caravaggio
(1571-1610)
Death of the Virgin
Italy, 1605-1606, oil on canvas,
369 x 245 cm.

The painting was commissioned by
a Vatican lawyer to decorate the altar
at his family chapel in a church in
Rome. It was acquired by Louis XIV
in 1671.

In the 17th century,
Caravaggio's monumental
compositions revolutionised
painting with their great
realism, which introduced
the most humble aspects of
everyday life into religious
depictions. Here, the death
of the Virgin is first and
foremost that of an
ordinary woman, whose
corpse lies simply on a bed,
her arm outstretched. The
intense dramatisation of
the scene, underlined by the
red theatrical curtain, gives
it a great deal of humanity
rather than sacredness,
emphasised by severe
contrasts between light and
shade, which would heavily
influence the Baroque and
Tenebrist tendencies.

▲ **99 Bartolomé Esteban Murillo** (1618-1682)
The Young Beggar
Spain, circa 1645-1650, oil on canvas, 134 x 110 cm.

This picture was part of the collection of King Louis XVI before entering the Louvre in 1782.

Caravaggio's influence spread as far as Spain, where the Tenebrist movement acquired a certain importance. Realism and chiaroscuro are united in this work depicting a young boy dressed in rags, feet black with dirt, sitting amid the crumbs of a frugal meal. The ray of sunshine lighting up the room draws attention to the gesture of this street child as he removes lice from himself, and thus gives this painting of daily life a very poetic feel.

▲ **100 Jusepe de Ribera** (1591-1652)
The Clubfoot
Spain, 1642, oil on canvas, 164 x 94 cm.

This painting was one of the 583 paintings left to the Louvre by Doctor Louis La Caze in 1869, in accordance with his will.

A young beggar is also the subject of this painting by Ribera, a Spanish painter based in Naples who was influenced by Caravaggio's work. However, the theatrical realism of the work is used for the purpose of social satire here. With his crutch, held proudly like a gun, his sign asking for charity ("Give me alms for the love of God"), his deformed foot and toothless mouth, this poor boy in fact apes the martial bearing of a Spanish officer: the cruel flipside of a period of great prosperity.

▶ **101 Guido Reni** (1575-1642)
Hercules defeats the Hydra of Lerna
Italy, 1617-1621, oil on canvas, 260 x 192 cm.

This painting is one of four pictures commissioned by Ferdinando Gonzaga. The series first featured in the collection of Charles I of England, then that of Everhard Jabach, a French financier and collector of German origin. Louis XIV bought his collection from him.

This work is part of a group of four pictures telling the story of Hercules; it shows one of twelve tasks that the demigod had to accomplish, killing the Hydra at Lerna Lake, a seven-headed serpent. The painting, showing the Baroque influence, incorporates chiaroscuro borrowed from Caravaggism and the twisting body which was a legacy of Mannerism, to develop the strength and vigour of the hero about to strike. This figure in suspension, captured in the moment, is typical of the innovations that the Baroque style brought to art in the 17th century, a summary of earlier developments.

◀ **102 Pierre Puget** (1620-1694)
Milo of Croton
France, circa 1670-1683, marble, 270 x 140 x 98 cm.

Commissioned by Colbert in 1670 for Louis XIV, this sculpture was placed in Versailles, first in the park then in the Special Museum of the French School. It was transferred to the Louvre in 1819.

The same ardour and same vigour captured in the moment, lending itself to the pattern of curves and folds, can be found in this sculpture by Pierre Puget, a Frenchman who learned the dynamic and dramatic power of Baroque art in Rome. Milo, an old athlete who had won the Olympic Games several times, wanted to prove his strength by trying to split a tree trunk with his hands. They got stuck and the man was held prisoner, unable to free himself to fight the wild beasts that preyed on him. The high tension and anxiety conveyed by the statue show the Baroque taste for theatre and emotional effects.

The century of Louis XIV

As a reaction to the Baroque movement, in France a "Classical" school emerged, favouring cold colours, straight lines, and rigorous, symmetrical compositions. The Antique inspiration that characterised the choice of subject was soon used for the purpose of glorifying King Louis XIV, who developed a vast iconographic programme and made art into a political manifesto.

▼ **103** **Nicolas Poussin** (1594-1665)
The Shepherds of Arcadia, **also called** *Et in Arcadia ego*
France, circa 1638-1640, oil on canvas, 85 x 121 cm.

Nicolas Poussin completely eschewed the Caravaggesque lighting and voluptuous shapes of Baroque art. On the contrary, he favoured an art of measure and balance, influenced by the rigour and order of the Antique model. In this work, a real manifesto of French Classicism, four young people in poses reminiscent of Greek statuary appear around a stone sarcophagus, in Arcadia. On it they are reading the engraved inscription *Et in Arcadia ego* ("Even in Arcadia, I [Death], exist") which gives philosophical meaning to a landscape imbued with great serenity.

▶ **104** **Nicolas Poussin** (1594-1665)
The Judgment of Solomon, France, 1649, oil on canvas, 101 x 150 cm.
This picture was painted by the banker Jean Pointel, an amateur and friend of Poussin in Rome. It entered the Louis XIV collection in 1685.

This picture shows an episode from the Old Testament: two mothers living under the same roof are arguing over the custody of a child and ask the King of Israel, Solomon, to pass judgment. He orders the baby to be cut in two so each woman can receive half of it. Poussin paints the moment when the soldier is about to execute the sentence. The real mother, on the left, prefers to give up her baby rather than see it die. The frontality of the composition, rigorous symmetry and attention paid to the tragic nature of the emotions give this work a Classical sense of harmony.

▶ **105** **Philippe de Champaigne** (1602-1674)
Ex-voto, France, 1662, oil on canvas, 165 x 229 cm.

The artist gave this picture to the Port-Royal convent in Paris, where it would be seized during the Revolution.

An *ex-voto* is an offering made to a deity in order to encourage them to grant a wish or thank them for a grace given. Here, the artist thanks God for healing his daughter, whose legs were paralysed, following prayers by the mother superior at Port-Royal convent, where the young girl was a nun. Champaigne depicts the two women with simplicity and a certain heaviness, in a sober setting that illustrates the Classical taste for order and measure.

▲ **106 Charles Le Brun** (1619-1690)
Chancellor Séguier
France, circa 1655-1661, oil on canvas, 295 x 357 cm.

Mentioned for the first time in 1764 at the home of one of the model's
descendents, this picture was seized during the Revolution. Its owners
retrieved it during the reign of Napoleon I and it remained with the Séguier
family until it was acquired by the Louvre in 1912, with the support of
the Friends of the Louvre.

In this equestrian portrait of Chancellor Pierre Séguier,
the state's number two administrator, we see the same taste
for simple settings and the same heaviness in the depiction
of the characters as in the ex-voto by Philippe de
Champaigne. Le Brun's picture is a reminder of the time
when Classical art was used by the ruling powers, in
the second half of the 17th century, making reference to
Antiquity - here, equestrian statuary. The rigour of this
pyramidal composition, like a formal ballet that the pages
seem to perform around the man of state, heralds the role
that Classicism would play during the reign of Louis XIV.

▶ **107 Antoine Coysevox** (1640-1720)
Fame riding Pegasus
France, 1699-1702, Carrara marble, 315 x 291 x 128 cm.

Moved to the Jardin des Tuileries in 1719 to restore a sense of prestige
to Louis XV's residence, the sculpture has been at the Louvre since 1786.
It has been replaced by mould of the original at the Tuileries.

Coysevox was one of the major figures in sculpture at
the court of Versailles: through equestrian statuary, he
exalted the greatness and majesty of royal power. This
Fame was commissioned for Marly Park, where the King
sometimes retired with a few of his courtiers. The scale
of this Pegasus, a winged horse and symbol of eternal
things, and its great expressive vigour give the sculpture's
Classical lines value as a political manifesto: the
sovereign's glory is announced by the small angel with
its trumpet.

▲ **108 Claude Gellée,
called Claude Lorrain** (1602-1682)
Seaport, Sunset
France, 1639, oil on canvas, 103 x 137 cm.

This painting belonged to André Le Nôtre, architect of
Louis XIV's gardens, who gave it to the King in 1693. It is a
replica of the picture painted in 1637 for Pope Urbanus VIII,
but in this version, the flags have fleurs de lys, emblems of
the King of France, and not bees, emblems of the Pope's
family, the Barberini.

Classical artists appreciated landscapes very
early on as a subject for idealised compositions
made up of real, historical and imaginary
elements. The rigour of the lines converging
towards the sunset and the gradation of warm
colours give the scene great serenity and
harmony. This apparent calm is troubled by
the many scenes taking place at the harbour, a
place of intense activity: men unload goods,
some play music while others fight.

French furniture
in the 17th and 18th centuries

In the 17th and 18th centuries, French furniture underwent a real revolution
in forms and techniques. For every monarch there was an easily identifiable style.
Lines were sometimes more graceful, sometimes straighter when the subjects
depicted reflected the tastes of the time.

▼ **109 André Charles Boulle** (1642-1732)
Wardrobe, France, circa 1700, ebony and amaranth veneer, marquetry with polychrome
woods, brass, tin, shell and horn, gilded bronze, 255 x 157 x 58 cm.

Although he did not invent it, the cabinet-maker Boulle made the best
use of the marquetry process that bears his name. This technique
consists of cutting a pattern out of two overlaid contrasting materials,
one light and one dark. The pattern made in one material is then
embedded in the background created by the other. Furniture produced
in this way combines a wide variety of materials in a dazzling array of
shell and brass, giving it an almost architectural dimension.

▶ **110 Charles Nicolas Dodin** (1734-1803)
and Martin Carlin (circa 1730-1785)
Pedestal table of Madame Du Barry
France, 1774, veneer, soft porcelain, 81.7 cm.

During the reign of Louis XV, French cabinet-making used not
only wood and bronze, but also lacquer and porcelain, as shown by
this pedestal table made by Dodin for the oval room at Madame
Du Barry's castle, in Louveciennes. The large circular plaque in
the middle, based on a painting by Van Loo showing three young
musicians performing for the Sultan, shows the century's
fascination with Turqueries. It is surrounded by six curvilinear
plaques based on paintings by Watteau, depicting romantic and
pastoral scenes.

▲ **111 Adam Weisweiler** (1744-1820)
Writing table of Queen Marie-Antoinette, France, 1784, ebony,
Japanese lacquer, mother-of-pearl, gilded bronze and steel, 73.7 x 81.2 x 45.2 cm.

The curved lines of the Louis XV style were followed by the
straight lines of the Louis XVI style. This writing table stood in the
inner cabinet of Marie-Antoinette at Saint-Cloud Castle in 1789.
It illustrates the taste for veneer and marquetry procedures of the
turn of the century during the Louis XVI period. This piece of
furniture in fact owes little to cabinet-making: the outside of the
table is mainly veneered with Japanese lacquer panels, depicting
Oriental-style landscapes. These highlight the fascination with
foreign lands of a century that was hungry for exoticism.

18th century:
A more intimate and decorative style of art

The 18th century was the time of the salons, held by aristocrats in the European metropolises to debate the great ideas of the century of philosophers and the Enlightenment. In these new spaces, art was more decorative and accompanied the changes and tastes of the time. It was also more intimate; romance and libertine love imbued the spirit of the century and led artists to take an interest in the most common sentiments.

▼**112 Francesco Guardi (1712-1793)**
Departure of the Bucentaure towards the Lido of Venice, on Ascension Day
Italy, between 1775 and 1780, oil on canvas, 67 x 101 cm.

This picture was part of a series of twelve depicting the ceremonies in Venice in 1763 for the election of the Doge Alviso IV Mocenigo. Ten of these pictures entered the Louvre in 1797 when they were seized by revolutionaries from the collection of the Count Depestre de Seneffe.

This work is typical of the art of *veduta*, a very detailed style of landscape painting featuring large urban panoramas. European aristocrats brought these images back as a souvenir of their travels in Italy, to display memories of their visit to Venice or Rome in their drawing rooms. Here, Guardi depicts the traditional Venetian Ascension Day ceremony, during which the Doge came out of his palace and took up his position on a parade ship, the *Bucentaure*, from which he threw a gold ring into the water, symbolising Venice's marriage to the sea.

▲ **113 Antonio Canal, called Canaletto** (1697-1768)
The Molo, Seen from the San Marco Basin
Italy, circa 1730, oil on canvas, 47 x 81 cm.

A *veduta* is a decorative image; in the 18th century, they adorned the intimate settings of aristocratic homes and reflected the period's taste for foreign lands. The Venetian painter Canaletto was undoubtedly the best at catering to this taste. He established himself in England very early on, where he produced a number of views of his birthplace. He began trading with rich customers who appreciated the great rigour of his perspectives, the soft light of his compositions and the great precision of his descriptions.

◀ **114 Daniel Govaers** (active in 1717)
Snuffbox
France, 1725-1726, gold, shell, diamonds, 3 x 8.5 x 6.5 cm.

As shown by the development of French furniture throughout the century, images gradually spread to places where they had never been seen before: painted portraits decorated all kinds of objects which were found in aristocrats' homes in the great European cities. This snuffbox made of gold, shell and precious stones has a portrait of the young Louis XV and his wife, Marie Leczinska, on the back of the lid, beneath crystal panels. It was given by the King as a diplomatic gift to Baron Cornelius Hop, the Dutch ambassador.

▶ **115 François Boucher** (1703-1770)

Lunch, France, 1739, oil on canvas, 81 x 65 cm.

The 18th century was soon inspired by the Dutch influence, inheriting its taste for depictions of indoor scenes; they were used to create an intimate atmosphere. This painting reveals the private world of a bourgeois family, perhaps the artist's, gathered around a cup of hot chocolate in a rich urban drawing room. With its fresh, romantic style, it also expresses the period's taste for happiness, as shown by the presence of children and their toys, which the painter Boucher sought to depict in each of his compositions.

▼ **116 Jean Baptiste Siméon Chardin** (1699-1779)

The Ray

France, circa 1725-1726, oil on canvas, 114 x 146 cm.

Chardin successfully presented *The Ray* and *The Buffet* for his admission to the Royal Academy. *The Ray* remained in its collections until its entry into the Louvre in 1793.

The 17th century in Holland still influenced Chardin, who distinguished himself in the still life genre as shown here. Far from Boucher's gracious style, this painting depicts the intimate setting of a kitchen, carefully arranged in a pyramid with the ray's head at the top. The mysterious animal, which seems to be looking at us, is opposed to life, embodied on the left by a small cat with its hair standing on end, and the immobility of inanimate objects on the right.

▼ **117 Antonio Canova**
(1757-1822)
Psyche Revived by Cupid's Kiss
Italy, 1793, marble, 155 x 168 x 101 cm.

In 1787, a Scottish colonel commissioned this group, which was finished in 1793. Murat, at the time King of Naples, bought it in Rome in 1801 for his castle in Villiers-la-Garenne. He sold it to his step-brother, Napoleon, in 1808. It was exhibited until 1822 at Compiègne Castle, before entering the Louvre.

The young Psyche was put into an eternal sleep by a spell cast by the goddess Aphrodite, jealous of her beauty. Cupid, the young girl's lover, awakened her by kissing her. The sculptor Canova captured the intimacy of this loving kiss in motion. Its depiction fits in with the century's taste for romantic things. However, the attention to ideal beauty, references to Antiquity and precise marble work already align the work with the budding Neoclassical movement.

Antonio CANOVA (1757-1822)

A new way of representing the individual

The great ceremonial portraits of the Classical era were followed by much more personal and psychological representations of individuals. Artists started to study the human feelings and characters of their model to give a kind of truth to their image. Far from the official poses, they show the spectator a man or woman in the intimacy of their age, thoughts or preoccupations.

▶ **118 Maurice Quentin Delatour** (1704-1788)
Portrait of the Marquise de Pompadour
France, 1755, pastel on blue paper, 175 x 128 cm.

In an exceptional format, this portrait is the most spectacular of all the pastels kept at the Louvre Museum. Delatour was able to satisfy his commissioner's wishes by giving her the image of a protector of the letters and arts: Louis XV's favourite, sitting at a table with several volumes on top of it, holds a music score in her hands. This official portrait is above all an intimate portrait where the marquise, in her home, is surrounded by familiar objects. Here, the portrait artist inaugurates a revival of the genre which was psychological as well as meaningful.

▶ **119 Jean-Baptiste Pigalle** (1714-1785)
Voltaire Nude
France, 1776, marble, 150 x 89 x 77 cm.

The first example of a statue created to celebrate a writer during his lifetime, this *Voltaire Nude*, far from idealising its model, shows an old man in all his physical decline: a skinny body, loose skin, prominent veins... It illustrates a new way of representing the individual that characterised the 18th century. Like in the *Portrait of the Marquise de Pompadour*, it strives to reveal the intimacy of its subject. The almost ecstatic expression on Voltaire's face seems to proclaim the triumph of the spirit over the fragility of the body.

▶ **120 Jean-Honoré Fragonard** (1732-1806)
Denis Diderot
France, circa 1769, oil on canvas, 82 x 65 cm.
This picture is part of a series of 14 "fantasy figures" that formed a portrait gallery in the lodgings occupied by Fragonard at the Louvre.

In the series called "fantasy figures", Fragonard depicts his friends and customers. With their upper body framed, wearing "Spanish-style" costume, the models lean on a stone ledge. Denis Diderot criticised his previous portraits for showing him in "the position of a Secretary of State, not a philosopher". The break away from ceremonial portraits was now complete: the Enlightenment philosopher is portrayed here with a book in his hand, with great vivacity.

▶ **121 Jean Antoine Watteau** (1684-1721)
Pierrot, formerly called *Gilles*
France, circa 1718-1719, oil on canvas, 185 x 150 cm.

Owned by Dominique Vivant Denon, Director of the museum under Napoleon I, this picture then belonged to Doctor Louis La Caze, who left his collection to the Louvre in 1869.

This portrait of Pierrot, a character from the commedia dell'arte, an Italian theatre genre which was very fashionable in Paris, replaced the formal representations of men of state with the naïve figure of a sad clown. The full-length portrait was a highly codified genre at the time; the artist used it in an unusual way and showed how a lunar character, surrounded by similarly surprising actors, could breathe new life into the representation of the individual.

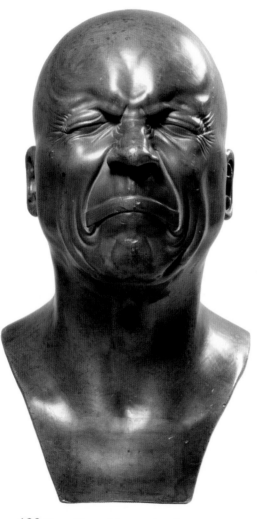

▲ **122 Franz Xaver Messerschmidt** (1736-1783)
Character head: Vexed Man
Germany, between 1770 and 1783, lead, H. 38 cm.

This work is part of the unique group of sixty-nine "Character heads" sculpted by the Austrian Franz Xaver Messerschmidt from the 1770s onward. Characterised by their various grimacing expressions, these heads each express a particular feeling: here, vexation. This sculptor's work, probably the most original of its time, illustrates the century's interest in more psychological representations of individuals, fitting in with the scientific research into character studies of the Enlightenment.

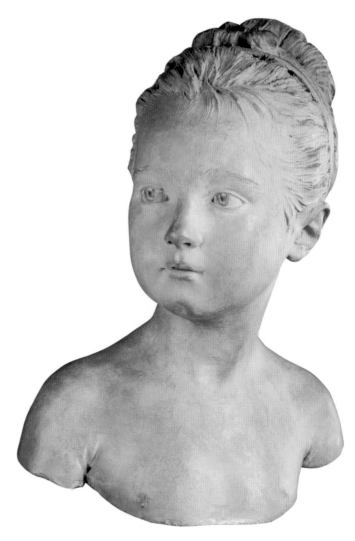

▲ **123** Jean-Baptiste Siméon
Chardin (1699-1779)
Self-Portrait at the Easel
France, 1779 (?), pastel on blue paper,
40 x 31 cm.

The author of *The Ray* made three
self-portraits using pastel during
the last ten years of his life; this
one seems to have been the last.
With his head wrapped in a white
cloth, he appears old and thin, with
a certain intimacy underlined by
the tight framing. This self-portrait
features the instruments of his
creation: his hand, a piece of red
pastel, the edge of an easel. This
was the last image he wanted to
leave for posterity: that of an artist
at work.

◀ **124** Jean Antoine Houdon
(1741-1828)
Louise Brongniart, aged five
France, 1777, terracotta, 35 x 24.2 x 24 cm.

This bust, exhibited at the Salon in 1777,
was frequently reproduced and copied.
The copy at the Louvre, acquired in 1898,
comes form the Brongniart family themselves.

The spontaneity of this portrait
and expressiveness of the child's
gaze show the desire to break away
from a certain heaviness in the
representation of the individual.
Houdon's model was the little
Louise Brongniart, daughter of
the architect Alexandre Théodore
Brongniart (1739-1813), who was
also responsible for the Palais de
la Bourse (stock exchange) built
during the time of Napoleon I,
between 1804 and 1815. At the
time, sensitivity manifested itself
in art, and more attention was paid
to the world of childhood.

▲ **125** Francisco de Goya y Lucientes (1746-1828)
The Countess del Carpio, Marquise of La Solana
Spain, 1794-1795, oil on canvas, 181 x 122 cm.

Carlos de Beistegui donated his prestigious painting collection to France in 1942. This picture entered the Louvre in
1953 after the donor's death.

Goya was the favourite portraitist of the Madrid nobility, who appreciated the acute sense
of psychological observation shown in his works. The Countess del Carpio, a cultured
aristocrat and playwright, knew she had a disease which she would die of by the year's
end. She appears prematurely aged, but her gaze remains firm. She looks at the spectator
proudly, while the latter can see her clarity in the face of the pain inside her.

19th century

The start of the 19th century was heavily steeped in Antique culture: the Neoclassicism and Empire style that developed under Napoleon constantly referred to the forms and taste of the ancient Romans, who glorified the values of order and courage. As a reaction to this, the Romantic painters, led by Delacroix, started a movement that aspired to greater freedom through expressive, lively and passionate compositions.

Eugène Delacroix (1797-1856)
The 28th of July.
Liberty guiding the people [detail]
France, 1830, oil on canvas, 260 x 325 cm.

The splendour of Empire

On 2 December 1804, at the Cathedral of Notre-Dame in Paris, Napoleon Bonaparte was crowned Emperor of the French. Thus began a period of ten years during which the new regime began producing art objects and artworks, which had been slowed down by the revolutionary events. References were frequently made to the Roman emperors and Charlemagne; this was aimed at legitimising the Emperor's power as well as exalting him.

▶ **126 Martin Guillaume Biennais**
(1764-1843)
Crown "of Charlemagne"
France, 1804, gilded copper, cameos, 25 x 18.5 cm.

The last emperor to have reigned over France was Charlemagne. Napoleon, preparing for his coronation, wanted to follow in the footsteps of the first Carolingian. For this reason, he commissioned this gilded copper crown from Martin Guillaume Biennais, which was intended to feature among the "Honours of Charlemagne", symbols of the new imperial power. It is adorned with cameos, mostly from a reliquary given to Saint-Denis Abbey by Jean, Duke of Berry, in 1401.

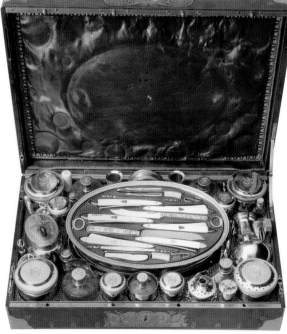

◀ **127 Martin Guillaume Biennais** (1764-1843)
Travel case of Napoleon I
France, 1806, mahogany, ebony (wood), crystal (material), ivory, marocain, mother-of-pearl.

This case arrived at the Louvre in 1969 as an anonymous donation.

The Emperor commissioned this travel case from his personal goldsmith, Martin Guillaume Biennais, who also made the *Crown "of Charlemagne"*, to give it to Czar Alexander I of Russia (1777-1825) in 1808. A travel case is a set of various utensils, contained in a precious portable case. This one contains stationery, grooming items and a tea service, with a total of around a hundred items.

▲ 128 Jacob Frères, based on
Louis Berthault's design
Bed of Madame Récamier

France, circa 1798, mahogany, bronze, bed: 100 x 133 x 100 cm,
stand: 138 x 200 cm.

This group of furniture decorated with swans, palmettos
and female statues adorned the bedroom of Madame
Récamier, wife of a rich banker, in her Parisian
mansion. The simple, sometimes imposing shapes, taste
for symmetry and Antique-style vocabulary of this
group already foreshadowed what would become the
"Empire style" of French furniture in 1798. It also
testified to the advent of a new social class that liked
to display its wealth, the bourgeoisie.

▶ 129 Sèvres Porcelain Factory
*The Battle of Eylau, panel designed to adorn the
pedestal of a "Cordelier" vase*

France, 1808-1810, hard porcelain, 51.5 cm.

This porcelain panel is part of a group of six, based on
the medals depicting Napoleon I's campaign in Prussia
and Poland in 1807, during which the French had to
fight the English, the Russians and the Prussians. This
one shows the Battle of Eylau, which was won by the
French on 8 February 1807. Napoleon is shown nude,
in the Antique style, sitting on cannons and weapons
taken from the enemy, in a profile view reminiscent of
the Roman emperors.

130 Jacques Louis David (1748-1825)

Coronation of Napoleon I, 2nd of December 1804 France, 1805-1808, oil on canvas, 621 x 979 cm.

Commissioned in 1804 by the Emperor and shown to the public in early 1808, the *Coronation* was exhibited at the Salon in the same year.
After Napoleon's marriage to Marie-Louise, in 1810, it was impossible to display the painting and David took it back into his studio.

In 1804, David was appointed First Painter of the Emperor, who commissioned him to paint four pictures to celebrate the coronation during which First Consul Bonaparte became Napoleon I. Only two of these paintings would finally be made, one of which was the *Coronation*, a magnificent composition with 191 characters. The scene takes place in the choir at the Cathedral of Notre-Dame in Paris. Wearing a crown of gold laurels, like the Roman

emperors, Napoleon has already been crowned and prepares to place the imperial crown on his wife Josephine's head. The composition is open enough to enable the spectator to take part in the event and recognise certain dignitaries of the Empire, marshals, members of the clergy and the Bonaparte family. This led the new Emperor to say: "This is not a painting, you can walk around in this picture!"

List of characters

On the floor, the marshals:

François Joseph Lefebvre carrying Charlemagne's sword; François Étienne Christophe Kellermann carries Charlemagne's crown; Catherine Dominique Perignon carries Charlemagne's sceptre; Géraud Christophe Michel Duroc; Jean Baptiste Bessières; Bon Adrien Jannot de Moncey; Jean de Dieu Soult; Joachim Murat; Jean Baptiste Jules Bernadotte carrying Napoleon's necklace; Louis Alexandre Berthier carrying the Emperor's globus cruciger on a cushion.

The Emperor

Originally, David had depicted Napoleon crowning himself, in order to symbolise the force and power of the event. He finally changed his mind and decided, in 1806, to show a "crowning" emperor who has already received the insignia of his new power. Cambacérès, a senator and state councillor, holds his main de justice (sceptre with a Hand of God as its finial).

Madam Mother

The Emperor had his own mother, Maria Letizia Ramolino (1750-1836), placed in the gallery in the painting, although she refused to attend the ceremony. This recasting of events shows how this image was used for political purposes by the authorities. Marshal Soult sits next to her.

The painter

Jacques Louis David depicts himself in the gallery, a witness to the coronation. By affirming his presence, he also appears as an influential supporter of the new regime. He is accompanied by other artistic figures, including his master, Joseph Marie Vien, Antoine Quatremère de Quincy, a member of the Institute, and Alexandre Lenoir, curator of the Museum of French Monuments.

And Napoleon's brothers and sisters:

Joseph Bonaparte
Louis Bonaparte
Caroline, called Murat
Pauline, called Borghese
Elisa, called Bacciochi.

In the ambassadors' gallery:

John Jr Armstrong,
ambassador of the United States
Ferdinando de Marescalchi, Italian ambassador
Mohamed Sayd-Halet Effendi,
ambassador of La Porte
Jean Philippe de Cobenzl, Austrian ambassador
Jérôme de Lucchesini.

The Pope

For the ceremony, Napoleon had the Pope Pius VII (1742-1823) brought over especially from Rome. As was customary, he was meant to place the crown on his head while administering the traditional sacraments. At the last moment, however, Bonaparte decided to crown himself and the Pope had to content himself with timidly blessing the new empire. Jean-Baptiste de Belloy, Cardinal Archbishop of Paris, is at his side.

Neoclassicism, Romanticism and new forms

The first half of the 19th century was marked by a great rivalry between two major artistic movements: Neoclassicism and Romanticism. The former advocated a return to the simplicity, purity and moral order of Antique art, while the latter tried to express the power of sensitivity, passions and imagination. These two movements would lead to the appearance of new forms that would have a considerable influence on all the Western artistic creation that followed.

▶ **131 Jacques Louis David** (1748-1825)
The Oath of the Horatii
France, 1784, oil on canvas, 330 x 425 cm.

Commissioned by the Count d'Angiviller for the directorate of the King's Buildings in 1784, this canvas can be seen in the Louis XVI collection.

As one of the first masterpieces of Neoclassical art, *The Oath of the Horatii* is its manifesto. The subject of the painting is taken from Roman history and shows the three Horatii brothers vowing to their father to defend the honour of the Romans, who have chosen them to challenge the Curiatii of Alba, an enemy town nearby. The great rigour of the composition in a simple setting revives a severe, moral art of lines, where sculptural figures in majestic poses express heroic sentiments.

◀ **132 Eugène Delacroix** (1798-1863)
The Death of Sardanapale
France, 1827, oil on canvas, 392 x 496 cm.

This picture was bought in 1921 from Baron Vitta thanks to the collector Maurice Audéoud, who had left his fortune to the Louvre in his will in 1899, to acquire artworks.

The subject of this painting refers to a tragedy by the English poet Byron: the Assyrian King Sardanapale, under siege in his capital, Nineveh, decided to kill himself rather than surrender. He decided to set fire to his palace so he could die with his treasures, women, horses and slaves. Rejecting the example of Greco-Roman Antiquity, and affirming the supremacy of colour and sinuous lines over the cold, rigid forms of Neoclassicism, this painting is one of the most brilliant illustrations of the Romantic movement.

▲ **133** **Jean Auguste Dominique Ingres** (1780-1867)
An odalisque,
called *The Great Odalisque*
France, 1814, oil on canvas, 91 x 162 cm.

Commissioned in 1813 by Caroline Murat, sister of Napoleon and Queen of Naples, this painting was never delivered because of the fall of Napoleon. It was bought by the Louvre in 1899.

Trained in the Neoclassical School at David's studio, which he ended up leaving, Ingres placed great importance on drawing in his compositions. Thus, he did not hesitate to add three additional vertebrae to his model in this painting, move her right breast and raise her left leg; all to emphasise the serpentine line that runs across this young harem woman's body and underline the great expressive qualities of her voluptuous form.

▶ **134** **Paul Delaroche** (1797-1856)
A Christian Martyr, Drowned in the Tiber during the Reign of Diocletian or *The Young Martyr*
France, 1855, oil on canvas, 170 x 148 cm

The children of Adolphe Seligman d'Eichtal, a banker and politician, left this picture to the Louvre in 1895, in accordance with their father's wishes.

This painting depicts a young Christian who lived in Rome during the reign of the Emperor Diocletian (245-313) and was thrown in the Tiber, her hands tied, for refusing to renounce her faith. While this picture's pathetic subject and chiaroscuro drama borrow heavily from the Romantic movement, its smooth, cold execution has more in common with the Neoclassical aesthetic. Delaroche played on this ambiguity throughout his career, and it brought him great success.

◄ 135 Eugène Delacroix (1797-1856)
The 28th of July, Liberty guiding the People
France, 1830, oil on canvas, 260 x 325 cm.

Bought at the Salon by the State in 1831, this painting was censored by Louis-Philippe. Hidden from the public for years, it entered the Luxembourg Museum in 1863, then the Louvre in 1874.

Here, Delacroix depicts a subject from contemporary history, the popular uprising of 27, 28 and 29 July 1830, which put an end to the reign of Charles X, brother of Louis XVI, in France. The painter was a witness to this event, which inspired him to produce this allegory of Liberty, a bare-chested young woman wearing the Phrygian cap, brandishing the tricolour flag and leading the people of Paris. You can see the enthusiasm that Romanticism showed for the revolutionary zeal of an era in love with liberty.

▶ 136 Théodore Géricault (1791-1824)
The Raft of the Medusa
France, 1819, oil on canvas, 491 x 716 cm.

Acquired by the Louvre in 1824 at a posthumous sale of Géricault's works.

Romanticism's taste for the pathetic aspect of the themes it addressed, dynamic compositions, highly realistic and sometimes crude description of the human body and the representation of despair and solitude culminate in this work by Géricault. It shows the shipwreck of the frigate *The Medusa*, in 1816, in which one-hundred-and-forty-nine passengers tried to escape by piling onto a raft. In the distance, a vessel approaches, the last hope of survival for this crew, whose depiction caused a scandal at the time.

▲ **137 Antoine Louis Barye** (1795-1875)
Lion and Snake
France, 1835, bronze melted with wax, 135 x 178 x 96 cm.

The Romantics appreciated the radical novelty of the sculptor
Barye's work, mainly dedicated to depicting the animal world.
These grand portrayals of wildlife were based on accurate scientific
knowledge and a certain epic feel that makes them very expressive.
Here, however, the work doubles as a political message, as
contemporaries saw the powerful figure of the lion as a discreet
tribute to the reign of Louis-Philippe.

▲ **138 Jean Auguste Dominique Ingres** (1780-1867)
The Turkish Bath, France, 1862, oil on canvas, 108 cm.

This painting was commissioned circa 1848 by Prince Napoleon, but he returned it to the
painter in 1860, as it shocked his wife, Princess Clothilde. Ingres reworked it and, in
1865, sold it to Khalil Bey, the former Turkish ambassador in St. Petersburg.

It then passed between the hands of various owners, before being
bought by the gallery owner Georges Petit in 1907, who sold it in
1911 to the Society of Friends of the Louvre.
This picture marks the end of Ingres' research into the female body
and Oriental exoticism, which had already been seen in *The Great
Odalisque*. Painted at the end of his career, it maintains its graphic
rigour, but immerses the spectator in a pile of overlapping bodies, with
surprising audacity. The dominant lines are the arabesques which
evoke a dialogue with Romanticism, as does the seraglio setting.

▲ **139 Caspar David Friedrich** (1774-1840)
The Tree of Crows (Baltic Sea Coast)
Germany, circa 1822, oil on canvas, 59 x 73 cm.

The Romantic taste rose in popularity in the Germanic countries
and the painting that developed there showed a new interest in
certain existential questions. In this painting by Friedrich, we can
see a tumulus - a kind of Celtic tomb made of earth - a bare,
tortured oak tree, and many crows: all these natural elements evoke
death, a necessary condition for accessing eternal life, symbolised
by the faraway land bathed in light.

▲ **140 Jean-Baptiste Camille Corot** (1796-1875)
Recollection of Mortefontaine
France, 1864, oil on canvas, 65 x 89 cm.

Acquired by Napoleon III at the Salon in 1864, then kept at Fontainebleau Castle until
1870, this picture was assigned to the national museums by a court ruling in 1879.

Here again, nature inspired the painter Corot to paint this
Recollection of Mortefontaine showing three characters picking fruit
in a forest near Paris. This universal theme depicts the integration
of humanity in its environment and animates this landscape with a
vaporous atmosphere. Baudelaire would hail Corot's work as a
"miracle of the heart and mind".

Tour of
20
remarkable places

In addition to its fabulous collections,
the Louvre is also a palace and museum housing
a wealth of rooms and exceptional decors
which deserve a visit in their own right.
Their history and their quality help to make
discovering the Louvre
an incomparable experience.

THE "NAPOLEON III APARTMENTS", Richelieu Wing, first floor

The Second Empire reception rooms

Between 1852 and 1857, Napoleon III had the current Richelieu wing constructed by his architects Louis Visconti and Hector Lefuel. There, among other institutions, he installed a library and the Ministry of State and of the Emperor's Household. For this latter administration, a suite of reception rooms was created, now known as the "Napoleon III Apartments". It includes several intimate rooms decorated with fine panelling in the 18th century style as well as an impressive series of official rooms. Their sumptuous decor was also inspired by the different decorative styles of the 18th century in France, where stuccos, marbles and gold dominated. The music room, surmounted by a gallery, was adorned with a large painting glorifying the Emperor. The spectacular Grand Salon could hold 250 people and be transformed into a theatre. The small and large dining rooms could be joined together on days when a large reception was held. The salons, which were occupied by the Finance Ministry between 1872 and 1989, have retained their decor and a large part of their original furniture.

THE MINISTER'S STAIRCASE
Richelieu Wing, ground floor

Sumptuous decor

THE MARLY COURT
Richelieu Wing, ground and lower ground floor

Works flooded with light

Leading from the internal courtyard, which was previously accessible to vehicles, to the 1st floor of the north wing of the Napoleon Court, it allows access to the Napoleon III Apartments. Its decor includes stone, coloured marble, golden bronzes and sculptures. Two large paintings by Charles Daubigny, one of the masters of the Barbizon School, adorn the upper part of the walls: they show the Pavillon de Flore and the Tuileries Palace. After the Commune, the staircase served the office of the Finance Minister.

When, between 1852 and 1855, the architects Visconti and then Lefuel created the Richelieu wing between the Napoleon Court and the Rue de Rivoli, they placed three different-sized courtyards in the centre of the area. The two largest, the Marly and Puget Courts, were placed towards the west and the smallest the Khorsabad, towards the east. The courts brightened up the building by providing the light necessary for the effective functioning of an essentially administrative building.

Originally open to the skies, the Marly Court provided vehicles with direct access to the foot of the Minister's Staircase. During the work to fit out this wing for the museum, in 1989 the Marly Court, like the two others, was covered with a glass roof designed by Ieoh Ming Pei, the architect who designed the Pyramid. With its roof, the Court became the largest space in the museum, in which some of the permanent collections of the Sculptures Department are displayed. All the

When contemporary art arrives at the museum

museum's works originating from the royal château in Marly, which no longer exists, are displayed there. These include the two groups of horses sculpted by Coysevox under Louis XIV and by Coustou under Louis XV, which originally adorned the drinking trough at Marly. Since 2011, there is also an arch dating back to the Renaissance era, which comes from the façade of the Tuileries. This is an interesting monument as it is directly linked to the history of the Louvre district.

The main staircase of the former Finance Ministry, previously known as the Library Staircase, opened onto the Richelieu passage. In addition to the Louvre Library which was on the second floor but destroyed under the Commune, it served several floors and mezzanine floors then used as offices, explaining its complexity. This monumental staircase, with its double flight of stairs, is lit by a number of bay windows which open onto both the exterior and the interior of the museum.

Highly mineral and with no painted decor, in 2010 it was supplemented with a series of works which had been entrusted to the artist François Morellet. The commission was part of the Louvre's policy to promote contemporary art and was an attempt to replicate the principle of major patronage operations carried out by the State. Morellet's work, a series of slightly destabilised windows, increases the number of perspectives of the real and fictitious apertures throughout the staircase.

THE "VEIL" OF THE VISCONTI COURT, Denon Wing

Islamic Arts

THE SUMMER APARTMENTS OF ANNE OF AUSTRIA
Denon Wing, ground floor

An incredible stucco decor

The most recently developed part of the Louvre is devoted to Islamic Arts and to the Eastern Mediterranean under the Roman Empire. It was inaugurated in September 2012 following four years of work. Located in the Visconti Court, of which they occupy the entire surface area over two floors, and framed by 17th and 19th century façades, the new areas are shaded by an undulating gold veil detached from the restored surrounding façades. Its architects, Rudy Ricciotti and Mario Bellini, covered it with a gold-coloured metallic membrane which glimmers in the light and provides a striking contrast with the mineral tones of the courtyard's perimeters.

For his mother, who suffered from the heat, in 1655 the young Louis XIV constructed new summer apartments facing not towards the south but towards the east. He placed them on the ground floor of the Petite Galerie. The stucco decor of this series of six rooms was entrusted to Michel Anguier and Pietro Sasso and the painting of the ceilings to Giovanni Francesco Romanelli. Occupied by the Council under the Regency, the rooms were then inhabited by a young Spanish infanta, the fiancée of Louis XV, who would give her name to the adjoining garden. The original spaces were considerably renovated as of 1799: the fitting out of the rooms for antiques brought back from Italy required the partitions to be removed from the rooms, which since then have only retained part of their ceilings.

THE SALLE DU MANÈGE
Denon Wing, ground floor

For a young prince

This room occupied the areas underneath the Salle des États. Accessible from the Lefuel Court via an elegant double ramp in the form of a horseshoe, this vast room was used as a riding room under the reign of Napoleon III. The animal-themed decor of its capitals recalls the original function of this room, which witnessed the first horse-riding attempts of the prince, the only child of the Imperial couple, who died tragically. A wooden platform allowed visitors to admire his progress. The riding room was given to the museum in 1879 and for a while housed the Museum of Plaster Casts. In 1989, the room was chosen to house restored antiques and copies of antiques.

THE SALLE DE DIANE
Denon Wing, ground floor

Royal Academy

The first "Salle de Diane" was created under Louis XIV to provide a better link between the old Louvre and the Petite Galerie, where the King constructed summer apartments for his mother, Anne of Austria. From 1712 to 1721, after the sovereign had left for Versailles, the room housed sessions of the Royal Academy of Painting and Sculpture. It was then possible to see the plaster casts of Hercule Farnèse, Laocoon and Flore Farnèse, reception pieces and portraits. Its current decor dates back to the renovation work carried out in the Neo-Classical style by the architects of Napoleon I. Its paintings are the work of Mérimée, Garnier and Prud'hon.

THE SAMOTHRACE STAIRCASE -
THE PERCIER AND FONTAINE ROOMS
Denon Wing, first floor

Art Deco simplicity

The museum's main staircase was renovated fairly recently. Designed for Napoleon III by Lefuel, it was intended to have a painted decor, which was never completed. It was Albert Ferran, sixty years later, who completed the current staircase, with its Art Deco simplicity, which leads to the Percier and Fontaine rooms, named after the architects who created them under Napoleon I. They originally formed the upper part of a staircase which gave access to the Salon Carré and then the Grande Galerie from the museum entrance. The stucco and painted decor, the marble columns and the sumptuousness of the ceilings recall this area's original role as main entrance.

THE SALON DENON
Denon Wing, first floor

To the glory of Napoleon III

This immense space occupies the central pavilion of the new south wing of the Louvre constructed by Napoleon III. Its height covers two floors and part of the huge attic area. Its painted, sculpted decor illustrates France, the fatherland of artistic creation, around figures of its main sovereigns who were patrons of the arts. These include Saint Louis, François I, Louis XIV and Napoleon I. In the centre, an allegorical figure of the Nation engraves the portrait of Napoleon III on a marble table, thus immortalising the glory of the Second Empire, which is placed on an equal footing with its illustrious predecessors.

The largest exhibition room in the world!

The largest room in the museum is a corridor originally 460 metres long; its only function was to provide a link between the Louvre Palace and the Tuileries Palace. Constructed under Henri IV starting in 1595, it was used as a setting for the fox hunts intended to amuse the young Dauphin! The decor of its vault, which Louis XIII entrusted to Nicolas Poussin, was never completed and only a few drawings now bear witness to this immense project. Occupied for a large part of the 18th century by the Plan-Relief Museum, now located at the Invalides, this site opened to the public during the Revolution and then housed the painting collections of the Museum of Arts. The Grande Galerie witnessed the marriage of Napoleon I and Marie-Louise, but had to wait two centuries to be completed. The current structure, consisting of a long space and a vault with overhead natural lighting emphasised by arches supported by groups of columns, dates back to the early 19th century. It was created by Percier and Fontaine, the Emperor's architects. Under Napoleon III, the gallery, which threatened to collapse, lost a third of its length. It nevertheless remains the largest exhibition room it is possible to visit.

THE GALERIE D'APOLLON Denon Wing, first floor

Begun by Le Brun in 1663 and completed by Delacroix in 1851

Louis Le Vau began construction of this gallery in 1661, on the site of the Galerie des Rois which Henri IV had wanted but which was destroyed by fire. Its painted decor was entrusted to Charles Le Brun, who began work on it in 1663 but abandoned the project fifteen years later to devote himself to his commissions at Versailles. In the 18th century, the Royal Academy of Painting and Sculpture, which was based at the Louvre, gave some of its members the task of completing the unfinished work, but it was Eugène Delacroix in 1851 who completed the gallery by finishing the painting of the central coffers of the vault.

GERMAIN PILON
1535   SCULPTEUR   1590

MICHEL ANDRE ANGUIER

ETIENNE DUPERAC

THE MEDIEVAL REMAINS
Sully Wing, lower ground floor

The Paris fortress

These are the oldest parts of the Louvre, surrounded by stonework some of which dates back to the late 12th or early 13th centuries. Today, it is possible to visit the sites previously invaded by water and which correspond to part of the north and east moats of the Louvre of Philippe Auguste. The stonework of the walls, in particular the Taillerie Tower (see below), still retains the marks made by the workers, the stone-cutters who were paid according to the number of blocks they worked in a day and who signed them to certify their work. The Saint-Louis Room (opposite) is the only medieval interior conserved at the Louvre.

THE SALLE DES CARIATIDES
Sully Wing, ground floor

16th century splendour

THE HENRI II STAIRCASE
Sully Wing, first floor

The oldest staircase in the Louvre

THE BRAQUE CEILING
Sully Wing, first floor

A 20th century painter

The most beautiful 16th century area of the Louvre was built on the orders of Henri II and completed in around 1555. The original hall had a wood-coffered ceiling enhanced with golden adornments. It was on the verge of ruin and was replaced under Louis XIII with the current stone vault, itself enhanced two centuries later with decorative reliefs sculpted at the request of Napoleon I. The hall bears the name of the four antique-style female figures sculpted by Jean Goujon, the Caryatids, used here for the first time in France and supporting the musicians' gallery. Although it was used for official festivities, in 1610 this area also housed a wax effigy of Henri IV.

Created by Henri II in 1549, this staircase is the oldest in the Louvre and one of the first examples in Renaissance France of a straight, not circular, staircase inside a building. It replaced a staircase planned by François I in the middle of the Lescot wing, but never completed. It went right to the top of the building and provided access to the upstairs guard room, the main access to the royal apartments. Its stone vault was decorated with motifs relating to hunting, one of the King's favourite pastimes and with Diana, an ancient divinity associated with him. The H, the monogram of Henri II, can be found repeatedly.

The wardrobe and antechamber of the King's apartments were located between the guard room and the sovereign's ceremonial room. It has formed just one large room since the time of Louis XIV in 1660 and retains part of its magnificent 16th century gilded wood ceiling: sculpted with the coat of arms of Henri II by Scibec de Carpi in collaboration with Etienne Carmoy, it was completed under the Sun King. In 1953, Georges Braque was entrusted with the creation of new paintings for the three roof coffers, whose decor had become damaged over time. *The Birds* was the first major example of 20th century art within the old palace walls.

THE SALLE DES BRONZES
Sully Wing, first floor

The Twombly ceiling

THE CHARLES X MUSEUM
Sully Wing, first floor

Terracotta and Greek vases

This vast hall was created under Henri II between 1549 and 1555. It was used as a guard room for the main access to the King's and Queen's apartments. It was here, on 24 October 1658, that Molière played for the first time in front of Louis XIV, who later held balls and festivities here. Under Louis XVIII, the room was transformed to host solemn opening meetings of sessions of chambers. It was renovated in 1930 by the architect Albert Ferran, who placed a low ceiling at an identical level to that of the 16th century and created windows facing the Napoleon Court and the Cour Carrée. The hall was given to the museum twenty years later and the Campana collections were displayed there from 1863 to 1869, then La Caze from 1869. Since 1936, the hall has housed antique bronzes and in 2010 it was given a new ceiling designed by the American Cy Twombly, who died in 2011.

Under the Restoration, the lack of exhibition space for the museum collections became particularly acute. The arrival of medieval and Renaissance works, and particularly the creation of Egyptian collections, forced Charles X to increase the surface areas open to the public. The series of rooms previously occupied by the Queen's apartments, on the first floor of the south wing of the Cour Carrée, was devoted

The monumental work by Kiefer

to the archaeology of Egypt and the Mediterranean. The plan was entrusted to Fontaine, while the furniture was created by Jacob-Desmalter. Several painters were entrusted with the ceilings, using themes linked to the collections on display: they mainly evoked Egypt and the Classical world. It was for one of these rooms that Ingres created *The Apotheosis of Homer*, which has now been replaced by a copy.

The internal work on the Colonnade wing, built under Louis XIV, was not completed until the early 19th century. It was Napoleon I who had Percier and Fontaine build the two monumental staircases which marked each of its extremities to the north and south. Their primary role was to serve the apartments which the King wanted to install in this location, thus taking up the major project not completed by

the Sun King. With only mineral decor, from the second half of the 19th century the north staircase was called the "Assyrian staircase". Since 2007, it has housed *Athanor*, a monumental work by the German Anselm Kiefer (who has lived in France since 1993), consisting of a painting and two sculptures, the first contemporary work created for the Louvre since Braque's *The Birds*.

Practical information

Louvre Museum
Main phone: 01 40 20 50 50
Information line: 01 40 20 53 17
Website: www.louvre.fr

Opening hours
The museum is open every day from 9am to 6pm, apart from Tuesdays, 1 January, 1 May and 25 December.
The rooms start to close at 5.30pm.
Wednesday and Friday evenings, late opening until 9.45pm (rooms start to close at 9.30pm).

Entry
Entry via the Pyramid and the Carrousel Gallery: open every day except Tuesdays from 9am to 7.30pm and until 10pm on Wednesdays and Fridays
Richelieu Passage: open every day except Tuesdays, from 9am to 5.30pm and until 6.30pm on Wednesdays and Fridays
Porte des Lions: closed on Tuesdays and Fridays. For opening hours on other days, call 01 40 20 53 17

Visitors without an entry ticket must use the Pyramid and Porte des Lions entrances (except on Fridays and late-opening evenings) and the Carrousel entrance.
Visitors with a ticket can use the reserved queue at the Pyramid entrance.
Visitors with cards (members, Friends of the Louvre, American Friends of the Louvre, teachers, partners and patrons) can use the Passage Richelieu entrance.
Visitors with disabilities or reduced mobility can use the priority entrance at the Pyramid.

Prices
Ticket for permanent collections: €11
Ticket valid the same day, for the Louvre museum, with the exception of the exhibitions in the Napoleon Hall, and the Eugène Delacroix Museum.
Ticket for exhibitions in the Napoleon Hall: €12
Ticket valid only for temporary exhibitions in the Napoleon Hall.
The free entry on the first Sunday of the month is not valid for exhibitions in the Napoleon Hall.
Combined ticket: €15
The combined ticket allows access to the permanent collections and to all the temporary exhibitions at the Louvre and the Eugène Delacroix Museum.

Exemptions
Free entry to the permanent collection of the Louvre Museum and the Eugène Delacroix Museum is granted on presentation of valid documentation for:
- under 18s
- young people from 18 to 25 who are resident in a country of the European Economic Area
- teachers with an Education Pass
- teachers of art history, history of art, visual arts and applied arts, who are employed, on presentation of documentation showing the subject taught.
- visual artists affiliated to the Maison des Artistes and the AIAP (International Association of Art)
- job seekers and those on income support (documentation less than a year old)
- visitors with disabilities and their accompanying person.

Free for everyone on the first Sunday of the month and 14 July (with the exception of the temporary exhibition in the Napoleon Hall).
Friday evenings from 6pm: free entry to the permanent collections for young people under 26 of any nationality on presentation of identification.

Free entry
Members of the Louvre Museum enjoy unlimited priority access to the permanent collections and, depending on their card, to the exhibitions in the Napoleon Hall.
All Louvre museum membership cards: http://www.louvre.fr/adhesions

Advance ticket sales
You may buy tickets in advance on the Internet, on the following networks:
- Fnac (tickets to permanent collections, exhibitions; auditorium tickets; cycles of workshops and conference visits)
- Ticketnet (tickets for permanent collections and exhibitions)
- Ticketweb (tickets for permanent collections and exhibitions)
Or by telephone:
Ticketnet:
From France: 0 892 390 100 (€0.34 inc. VAT/min) or from abroad: +33 (0)1 46 91 57 57
Fnac:
From France: 0 892 684 694 (€0.34 inc. VAT/min) or from abroad: +33 (0)1 41 57 32 28
Note: these tickets cannot be collected at the Louvre Museum.

LOUVRE MUSEUM

President-Director
Henri Loyrette

General Administrator
Hervé Barbaret

Assistant General Administrator
Claudia Ferrazzi

Director of Cultural Production
Juliette Armand

Louvre Museum
75058 Paris cedex 01
www.louvre.fr

THIS GUIDE IS A PUBLICATION CO-EDITED BY THE LOUVRE MUSEUM AND TTM ÉDITIONS

Editors
Violaine Bouvet-Lanselle, Louvre Museum, and Claude Pommereau, TTM Éditions

Editorial coordinator Laurence Castany

Artistic Direction Bernard Borel

Graphic Design Xavier Henry

Iconography Florelle Guillaume

Editing Secretary Franck Antoni

© Musée du Louvre, 2012
ISBN : 978-2-84278-950-3
© Beaux Arts/ TTM Éditions, 2012
ISBN : 978-2-84278-934-3
Copyright: August 2012
Photoengraving: Litho Art New, Turin
Printing: Clerc, Saint-Amand Montrond [Print in France]

BEAUX ARTS ÉDITIONS

Beaux Arts Éditions are published by TTM Éditions.

Manager
Thierry Taittinger

Distribution Manager
Florence Hanappe

Distribution to bookshops
CLIENTS UD
Flammarion distribution
commandesclients@union-distribution.fr
Tel 01 41 80 20 20

Other bookshops
Mathilde Alliot
Tel 01 41 08 38 06

Beaux Arts / TTM Éditions
3, Carrefour de Weiden
92130 Issy-les-Moulineaux - France
RCS Paris B 435 355 896

AUTHORS

Barthélemy Glama : p. 22-23 and 48-139.
Claude Pommereau : p. 20-21 and 26-27.
Daniel Soulié : p.8-19, 24-25, 28-47 and 140-153.

BIBLIOGRAPHY

Geneviève Bresc-Bautier, *The Louvre, a Tale of a Palace*, coed. Musée du Louvre Éditions / Somogy
Collectif, *L'histoire du Louvre*, 3 volumes, coed. Musée du Louvre Éditions/Fayard (2013)

ACKNOWLEDGEMENTS

Alexandra Buffet, Chrystelle Meyer, Alexandrine Stehelin, Donato di Nunno.

How to reach the museum

Metro: lines 1 and 7, Palais-Royal/Musée du Louvre station.
Bus: no 21, 24, 27, 39, 48, 68, 69, 72, 81 and 95
Vélib' stations close to the museum:
n°1015: 2 place A. Malraux, n°1023: 165 rue Saint-Honoré, n°1014: 5 rue de l'Échelle, n°1013 : 186 rue Saint-Honoré.
Car: an underground car park can be accessed via Avenue du Général Lemonnier, every day from 7am to 11pm.
Batobus: Louvre, Quai François-Mitterrand stop

Services

Loans of equipment: folding stools, pushchairs, baby-carriers and wheelchairs are available to visitors free of charge at the information centre in the Napoleon Hall, in exchange for identification.
Cloakrooms and left-luggage: the museum has cloakrooms which are free with your museum entrance ticket or documentation; small lockers are also available.
The cloakrooms under the Pyramid are open every day except Tuesdays, from 9am to 6.45pm and until 9.45pm on Wednesdays and Fridays.

Louvre Audioguide – Nintendo 3DS™
The audioguide is available in 7 languages: French, English, Spanish, Italian, German, Japanese and Korean.
These can be found at the cash desks and automatic distributors.
They can be obtained in exchange for an identification document at the dedicated counters located under the Pyramid and at the Denon, Sully and Richelieu entrances.
Full price: €5 / Solidarity and young people price: €3 / Free for 3 children with the Louvre Families card.

Buying tickets for the Louvre auditorium

Information: 01 40 20 55 55,
from Monday to Friday from 9am to 7pm.
www.louvre.fr
Reservations:
01 40 20 55 00, from Monday to Friday (except Tuesdays) from 11am to 5pm, payment by bank card only.
At the Auditorium cash desk:
from Monday to Saturday (except Tuesdays) from 9am to 5.30pm.

Workshops and visits

Different types of assisted visits are available for museum visitors: conference visits, architectural walks, workshops for children and adults, etc.
Information: 01 40 20 52 63
Bookings: 01 40 20 51 77

Eugène Delacroix National Museum

6, Rue de Furstenberg, 75006 Paris
Open every day except Tuesdays, from 9.30am to 5pm.
Access: metro Saint-Germain-des-Prés (line 4) or Mabillon (line 10)
Information: 01 44 41 86 50
Permanent collections: €5
Temporary exhibitions: €7
Combined Louvre-Delacroix ticket: €15, valid for the day of purchase for visits to the permanent collections.

Tuileries Gardens

Open from 7.30am to 7.30pm in winter and from 7am to 9pm in summer.

Become a museum member

Different membership cards and passes for the Louvre are available in the "membership area", in the Carrousel Gallery.
Every day, except Tuesdays, from 9am to 5.15pm and until 9pm on late-opening evenings.
Tel: 01 40 20 51 04
Download membership brochures from www.louvre.fr

Young Person's Louvre card

For those aged under 30
adhesion.louvrejeunes@louvre.fr

Louvre Professionals card
louvreprofessionels@louvre.fr

Louvre Families card
adhesion.louvrefamilles@louvre.fr

Join the Society of Friends of the Louvre

The Society of Friends of the Louvre is an association independent of the Louvre Museum.
Free, permanent access to the museum and temporary exhibitions.
Individual membership information:
01 40 20 53 34/53 74
Information for groups:
01 40 20 84 94
Information on Friends of the Louvre:
01 40 20 53 34 or 01 40 20 53 74
www.amis-du-louvre.org
Friends of the Louvre counter in the Carrousel Gallery (Allée du Grand-Louvre) open every day except Tuesdays and Sundays from 10am to 5.30pm.

Lower ground floor

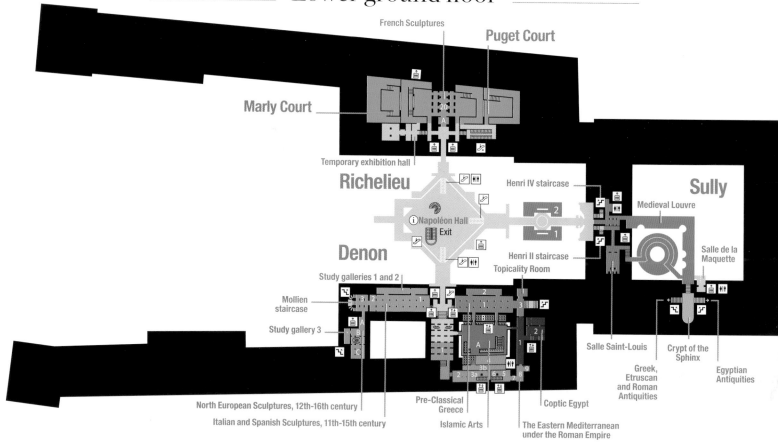

French Sculptures

Puget Court

Marly Court

Temporary exhibition hall

Richelieu

Henri IV staircase

ⓘ Napoléon Hall
Exit

Sully

Medieval Louvre

Salle de la Maquette

Denon

Study galleries 1 and 2

Mollien staircase

Study gallery 3

Henri II staircase

Topicality Room

Salle Saint-Louis

Crypt of the Sphinx

Greek, Etruscan and Roman Antiquities

Egyptian Antiquities

North European Sculptures, 12th-16th century

Italian and Spanish Sculptures, 11th-15th century

Pre-Classical Greece

Islamic Arts

Coptic Egypt

The Eastern Mediterranean under the Roman Empire

Ground floor

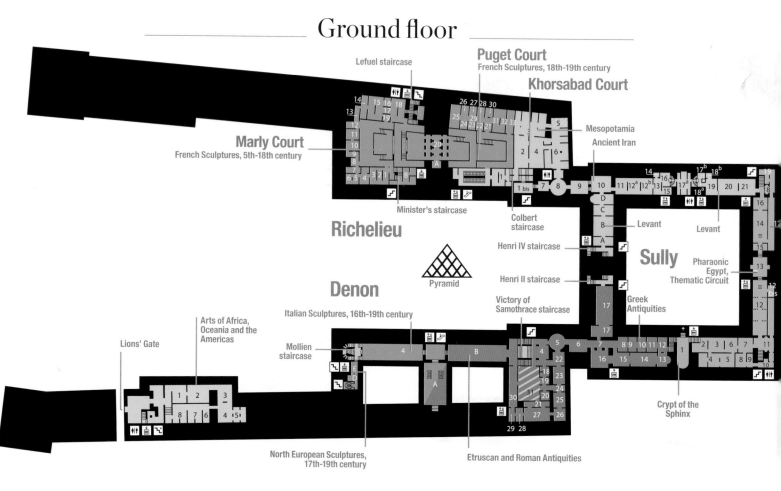

Lefuel staircase

Puget Court
French Sculptures, 18th-19th century

Khorsabad Court

Marly Court
French Sculptures, 5th-18th century

Mesopotamia

Ancient Iran

Minister's staircase

Richelieu

Colbert staircase

Henri IV staircase

Levant

Levant

Pyramid

Sully

Henri II staircase

Pharaonic Egypt, Thematic Circuit

Denon

Italian Sculptures, 16th-19th century

Victory of Samothrace staircase

Greek Antiquities

Arts of Africa, Oceania and the Americas

Lions' Gate

Mollien staircase

North European Sculptures, 17th-19th century

Etruscan and Roman Antiquities

Crypt of the Sphinx

Decorative Arts   Paintings   Prints and Drawings   Sculptures   Near Eastern Antiquities   Egyptian Antiquities   Islamic Arts   Greek, Etruscan and Roman Antiquities

1rst floor

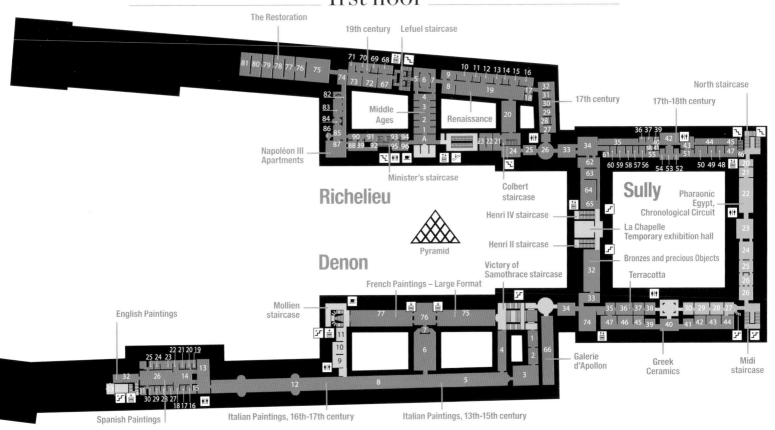

The Restoration

19th century · Lefuel staircase

81 80 79 78 77 76 · 75

82
83
84
86 85
87 · 90 91 93 94
88 89 92 · 95 96

74 73 72 67

5 6 7
4
3
2
1
A

71 70 69 68

10 11 12 13 14 15 16
9
8
19

17
18

32
31
30
29
28
27

Middle Ages

Renaissance

20

23 22 21

24 · 25 · 26

33

34

61

35

36 37 39
38 41
55
60 59 58 57 56

40
42
54 53 52

17th century

17th-18th century

North staircase

44 45
43 46
51 47
50 49 48

Sully

20
21
22
23
24
25
26
26

Napoléon III Apartments

Minister's staircase

Colbert staircase

Henri IV staircase

Henri II staircase

Victory of Samothrace staircase

Richelieu

Denon

Pyramid

62
63
64
65

32

33

Pharaonic Egypt, Chronological Circuit

La Chapelle Temporary exhibition hall

Bronzes and precious Objects

Terracotta

34

74

35 36 37 38
47 46 45
39

30 29 28 27
31
40
41 42 43 44

Greek Ceramics

Midi staircase

English Paintings

Mollien staircase

French Paintings – Large Format

32
33

25 24 23

22 21 20 19

13
26 · 14
15
30 29 28 27
18 17 16

77

76

75

11
10
9

1
4 · 2
3
66

6
8
5

Galerie d'Apollon

Spanish Paintings

Italian Paintings, 16th-17th century

Italian Paintings, 13th-15th century

2nd floor

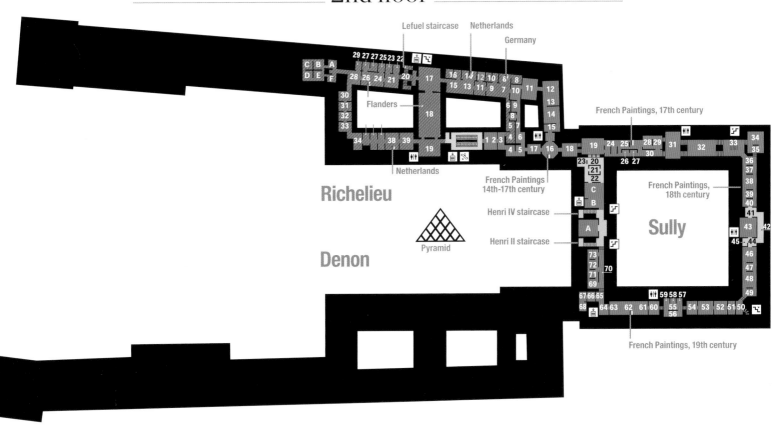

Lefuel staircase · Netherlands

Germany

29 27 27 25 23 22

C B A
D E
F

28 26 24 21
20

30
31
32
33

34

38 39

17

16 14 12 10
15 13 11 9

8 7
6
5

11

12
13
14
15

Flanders

18

19

1 2 3 4

French Paintings, 17th century

34
35

36
37
38
39
40
41

43
45 44

46
47
48
49

Netherlands

French Paintings 14th-17th century

Henri IV staircase

Henri II staircase

16 17
18

19 24 25
26 27

28 29
30

31 · 32 · 33

23 20
21
22

C

B

A

73
72
71
69

70

67 66 65
68 · 64 63 62 61 60

Richelieu

Denon

Pyramid

Sully

French Paintings, 18th century

59 58 57

55
56
54 53 52 51 50

French Paintings, 19th century

The numbers on all the plans are those of the rooms of the Louvre.

157

The Department of Islamic Art, reopened on September 2012
in new galleries in the Cour Visconti. © MUSÉE DU LOUVRE, DIST. RMN / PHILIPPE RUAULT, © R. RICCIOTTI - M. BELLINI / MUSÉE DU LOUVRE